IMPROVEMENT SERVICE MARKET STRATEGIES

JOHN LOK

Copyright © John Lok
All Rights Reserved.

Contents

Preface

This book is a business psychological teaching book. This book aims to indicate some sample different kinds of client individual psychological emotion challenges to give opions to let these businesses how to solve these psychological challenges and how to attract clients' concerning to their products or services. Also, I shall explain how to use psychological methods to predict clients' emotion in order to attract more clients to choose to use these businesses' services or buy these businesses' products. These product or service businesses include space exploration relative product, natural energy resource product, environment pollution product, road transportation design service, airline fuel product, Disney entertainment service, travel agent service, education service etc. I feel any businesses can keep longer time to grow up if businessmen can know how to use psychological methods to predict their clients' positive emotions. I shall give my opinions to answer how to predict these businesses' client emotion, such as how Disney can attract more visitors; how to predict clients' emotion to consume space travel entertainment and/or space relative products; how to increase student numbers, how to predict traveller individual's travelling destination choice etc. client psychological choice behaviors.

I write this book aim to let readers to raise knowledge how to predicts service industries consumers needs and research what factors can influence their needs change.

The first market concerns travel industry: How to predict future travel behaviour from past travel behaviour for travel agents benefits. I shall indicate how to predict travel behavioural consumption from psychology view and computer statistic both view points and qualitative of travel behavioural method to achieve how to operate travel business more successfully.

The second market concerns school education industry. I shall indicate what the factors can influence the final grades of academic students. I shall give examples to explain why these factors can influence the final grades to be bad of academic students easily. Those factors include: tutoring method factor, class attendance and academic performance factor, drinking and academic motivation factor, the link between sleep quantity and academic performance factor, the relationship between physical fitness and academic performance factor, the relationship between student's learning style and academic performance factor as well as the relationship between time management and academic performance total seven factors.

The third market concerns outsourcing either manufacturing or service strategy. Although, nowadays, outsourcing is popular strategy to any global organizations. But they neglect outsourcing strategy has also disadvantages. I shall explain why outsourcing strategy can bring benefits to some organizations, but it can also bring disadvantages to some organizations. I shall indicate evidences to explain what the reasons are not right when the organizations choose outsourcing strategy. I shall explain why any organizations need to analyze their situations whether are suitable to apply outsourcing strategy to operate their management, before they decide to make outsourcing strategy.

The fourth market concerns multi-level market. Pyramid scheme of the economic analysis of the criteria is used to distinguish what the difference is multi level marketing sale channel and direct personal sale channel . I shall utilize economy theory in reaching the opinion what the difference view points were between direct personal sale and multi level marketing, toward determining whether the reasoning can also generate false positive. I also discuss the welfare implications of different tests that might be used to distinguish a legitimate direct seller (pyramid scheme) and multi-level marketing from a fraud. The, I shall dicate the different types of consumer frauds by calculation and considerations which both employ to detect whether pyramid and personal direct sale fraud both are occurring. Finally, I shall explain whether Multi-Level Marketing can assist global economic growth in our societies.

The fifth market concerns travelling road driving market. I shall explain why it has close relationship between travellers number influence and the crisis of road traffic fatalities to any countries. I shall indicate Japan travellers' road driving behaviors. I shall apply rational choice theory to explain why drinking alcohol of drivers' behaviours can cause Japan's economic development indirectly. I shall give reasons to explain different country government's transportation and travel development departments ought need to concern their traveller road driving behavior how to influence their traveller visitor numbers.

The six market concerns MTR (underground train) transportation strategy. I shall explin why MTR underground train transportation needs to know passenger behaviour. What are the factors to cause passengers who choose to catch other transportation tools? Indicating methods how to solve passenger choice challenges to attact many passengers who will choose MTR to catch more than other kind of transportation tools. It is suitable to any readers who have interest to learn how to use transportation behaviour strategy to solve passenger behavioural choice.

The seven market concerns airline market. I shall let economic students who can learn how to use behavioral economic method to solve the fuel price rising risk to global airline industry. Also I hope any airline company management leader who can learn how to apply behavioral economic method to predict when fuel price rising to avoid its risk and how to avoid the fuel price rising bad influence to cause whose airline businesses failure for long term. Finally, I shall indicate what factors cause the fuel price will raise as well as I shall indicate what the other external threats can cause risk to airline industry and I shall also compare the fuel price rising factor and other external threats whether which is the most effort to influence airline industry failure. Then, I shall give recommend how global airline industry can apply behavioral economic method to avoid the fuel price rising bad influence.

The eight market concerns space technological industry. I shall indicate what space business's benefits will be contributed to human . I shall research whether what economic factors are influenced to our daily living by the space business main country players. Awareness of the space industry is critical of public policy is to support it. As the impact of climate change makes survival for the human species increasingly problem, the imperative to develop the means to evacuate planet Earth and sustain human existence becomes critical. The first chapter explains a conceptualization exploration of space how is presented from a globalization perspective. The Second chapter indicates what the benefits are managed to international cooperation in space exploration. The third chapter indicates the impact of space exploration activities upon society. The final chapter indicates the benefits stemming from space exploration. I shall provide a comprehensive review of how space technology can be used to resolve fundamental environmental, technological, and humanitarian challenges that we are experiencing on our planet.

This book final market concerns foods and product manufacturing market. I shall indicate how to predict customer' emotion to judge whether how to produce or design your foods or products to sell to them successfully. I want to give my opinions to let businessmen to know how to
predict consumer emotion to avoid the risk to spend excess investment to

invent the new products or produce the bad taste foods or soft drinks to promote to enter to sell wrongly. I shall use three science and psychology methods to explain what suitations your products or foods can sell from online more acceptable. So, this book teach students to learn how to use the suitable strategies to achieve to manage any business more success. In my this books which indicate some business concepts and theories how to apply to these kind of buiness markets to achieve more accurate strategical methods effectively.

Prologue

- How to use qualitative of travel behavioural method to predict future travel consumption.

  - How to apply advanced traveler information systems (ATIS) to predict future travelling behaviour.

  - How does online tourism sale channel can influence traveling consumption of behaviour.

- Actively based patterns of urban population of travel behavioural prediction method.

  - What is trip based versus activity based approaches?

- Why senior age will be main travelling target.

  - How to psychological method to predict travel behavioural consumption.
  - Bibliography

Chapter 3
SCHOOL EDUCATION MARKET

- Tutoring method factor p.72-102
  Reading habits among students and its effect on academic performance factor

- Class attendance and academic performance factor

- Drinking and academic motivation factor

- The link between sleep quantity and academic performance factor

- The relationship between physical fitness and academic performance factor
- The relationship between student's learning style and academic performance factor
- The relationship between time management and academic performance factor

Chapter 4
Ecommerce Multi-Level Service marketing

- What are the differences between multi level marketing and direct personal sale? p.104-126

- Whether multi level marketing can assist economic growth.

- Why the internet has positive influence on direct sale industry in multi level market to assist economic growth.

- Whether multi level marketing can influence economic growth in poverty countries.

Chapter 5
MTR (UNDERGROUND TRAIN) TRANSPORTATION
SERVCE MARKET

- Why MTR underground train transportation needs to know passenger behaviour. p.127-138
- Why route choice can influence passenger
- behavioural choice.
- Why trip time reliability and crowding factors can influence MTR passenger choice.
- What is the crowding difference between train and MTR underground train.
- How MTR can attract many passengers.

ONE

HOW APPLYING ECONOMY THEORIES SOLVE SERVICE MARKET CONSUMER BEHAVIORS

In service market, we can apply demand and supply theory to solve some service market consumer behaviors.The economic problem – sometimes called the basic or central economic problem – asserts that an economy's finite resources are insufficient to satisfy all human wants and needs. Economics involves the study of how to allocate resources in conditions of scarcity However, viewing economics as the study of how society allocates resources can lead to conflation of normative economic planning and empirical study of how economic agents operate in these conditions.

In mainstream neoclassical economics, it is assumed that humans pursue their self-interest, and that the market mechanism best satisfies the various wants different individuals might have. These wants are often divided into individual wants (which depend on the individual's preferences and purchasing power parity) and collective wants (which are the wants of entire groups of people). Things such as food and clothing can be classified as either wants or needs, depending on what type and how often a good is requested.

However, economists have sometimes characterized "how" to produce as a "technological problem" of efficiency whereas the allocation of what is produced is an "economic problem". In a free market, the "how" of production and allocation of resources is distributed among economic agents. In a centrally planned economy, a principal decides how and what to produce on behalf of agents. Modern economies are often welfare capitalist with various regulations, which makes the economic system more equitable while retaining the distributed free market system. Due to human wants are unlimited, an infinite series of human wants remains continue with human life. Nobody can claim that all of his wants have been satisfied and he has no need to satisfy any further want. Everybody feels hunger at a time then other he needs water. Sometime one feels the desire of clothing then starts to feel the desire of having good conveyance. When all existing wants are satisfied then new wants starts to create in mind, so the series of wants remains continue till the last moment of life. So an economic problem arises because of existence of unlimited human wants.

● Problem of allocation of resources

The problem of allocation of resources arises due to the scarcity of resources, and refers to the question of which wants should be satisfied and which should be left unsatisfied. In other words, what to produce and how much to produce. More production of a good implies more resources required for the production of that good, and resources are scarce. These two facts together mean that, if a society decides to increase production of some good, it has to withdraw some resources from the production of other goods. In other words, more production of a desired commodity can be made possible only by reducing the quantity of resources used in the production of other goods.

The problem of allocation deals with the question of whether to produce capital goods or consumer goods. If the community decides to produce capital goods, resources must be withdrawn from the production of consumer goods. In the long run, however, [investment] in capital goods augments the production of consumer goods. Thus, both capital and consumer goods are important. The problem is determining the optimal production ratio between the two.

In fact, in our societies, resources are scarce and it is important to use them as efficiently as possible. Thus, it is essential to know if the production and distribution of national product made by an economy is maximally

efficient. The production becomes efficient only if the productive resources are utilized in such a way that any reallocation does not produce more of one good without reducing the output of any other good. In other words, efficient distribution means that redistributing goods cannot make anyone better off without making someone else worse off. (See Pareto efficiency.) So, scientists will apply efficient distribution methods to help any countries to earn the absolute advantages when we buy and sell any kinds of products or food between ourselves countries, e.g. when US has good natural resource to grow any food, e.g. potato, wheat , vegetable, cotton , then US can export to sell to China, because China has no any farms to grow agriculture food to supply itself Chinese to eat. So, China must need to buy any agriculture food from US. Otherwise, China has cheap labor to supply to US any manufacturers to help them to manufacture their electronic products. SO, it has many US factories are built in China to let Chinese workers help them to produce their products because their wages are cheaper to compare US workers. So, comparative economic advantage will be choice to apply between US and China both countries. (Absolute advantage trade theory)
The inefficiencies of production and distribution exist in all types of economies. The welfare of the people can be increased if these inefficiencies are ruled out. Some cost must be incurred to remove these inefficiencies. If the cost of removing these inefficiencies of production and distribution is more than the gain, then it is not worthwhile to remove them.

● The problem of full employment of resources
In view of how to use available resources are fully utilized is an important one. A community should achieve maximum satisfaction by using the scarce resources in the best possible manner—not wasting resources or using them inefficiently. There are two types of employment of resources:
(1) Labour-intensive
(2) Capital-intensive
In capitalist economies, however, available resources are not fully used. In times of depression, many people want to work but can't find employment. It supposes that the scarce resources are not fully utilized in a capitalistic economy.
● The problem of economic growth
If productive capacity grows, an economy can produce progressively more goods, which raises the standard of living. The increase in productive

capacity of an economy is called economic growth. There are various factors affecting economic growth. The problems of economic growth have been discussed by numerous growth models, including the Harrod-Domar model, the neoclassical growth models of Solow and Swan, and the Cambridge growth models of Kaldor and Joan Robinson. This part of the economic problem is studied in the economies of development.

● Needs and wants problems

Needs are things or material items of peoples need for survival, such as food, clothing, housing, and water. Everyone has a different needs and wants. Until the Industrial Revolution, the vast majority of the world's population struggled for access to basic human needs.

Wants are effective desires for a particular product, or for something that can only be obtained by working for it. While the fundamental needs of survival are key in the function of the economy, wants are the driving force that stimulates demand for goods and services. To curb the economic problem, economists must classify the nature and different wants of consumers, as well as prioritize wants and organize production to satisfy as many wants as possible.

● Five bases problems of economy

In our societies , in general, our societies will have these similar problems The following points highlight the five basic problems of an economy. The problems are: 1. What to Produce and in What Quantities? 2. How to Produce these Goods? 3. For whom is the Goods Produced? 4. How Efficiently are the Resources being utilized? 5. Is the Economy Growing?.

Problem 1:What to Produce and in What Quantities?
The first central problem of an economy is to decide what goods and services are to be produced and in what quantities. This involves allocation of scarce resources in relation to the composition of total output in the economy. Since resources are scarce, the society has to decide about the goods to be produced: wheat, cloth, roads, television, power, buildings, and so on. Once the nature of goods to be produced is decided, then their quantities are to be decided. How many tones of wheat, how many televisions, how many million of power, how many buildings, etc. Since the resources of the economy are scarce, the problem of the nature of goods and their quantities has to be decided on the basis of priorities or preferences of the society.

If the society gives priority to the production of more consumer goods now, it will have less in the future. A higher priority on capital goods implies less consumer goods now and more in the future. But since resources are scarce, if some goods are produced in larger quantities, some other goods will have to be produced in smaller quantities. Suppose the economy produces capital goods and consumer goods. In deciding the total output of the economy, the society has to choose that combination of capital goods and consumer goods which is in keeping with its resources.

Problem 2: How to Produce these Goods?

The next basic problem of an economy is to decide about the techniques or methods to be used in order to produce the required goods. This problem is primarily dependent upon the availability of resources within the economy. If land is available in abundance, it may have extensive cultivation. If land is scarce, intensive methods of cultivation may be used. If labour is in abundance, it may use labour- intensive techniques; while in the case of labour shortage, capital-intensive techniques may be used.

The technique to be used also depends upon the type and quantity of goods to be produced. For producing capital goods and large outputs, complicated and expensive machines and techniques are required. On the other hand, simple consumer goods and small outputs require small and less expensive machines and comparatively simple techniques.

Further, it has to be decided what goods and services are to be produced in the public sector and what goods and services in the private sector. But in choosing between different methods of production, those methods should be adopted which bring about an efficient allocation of resources and increase the overall productivity in the economy.

Problem 3. For whom is the Goods Produced?

The third basic problem to be decided is the allocation of goods among the members of the society. The allocation of basic consumer goods or necessities and luxuries comforts and among the household takes place on the basis of among the distribution of national income. Whosoever possesses the means to buy the goods may have then. A rich person may have a large share of the luxuries goods, and a poor person may have more quantities of the basic consumer goods he needs.

Problem 4: How Efficiently are the Resources being Utilised?

This is one of the important basic problems of an economy because having made the three earlier decisions, the society has to see whether the resources it owns are being utilized fully or not. In case the resources of the economy are lying idle, it has to find out ways and means to utilize them fully.

Problem 5: Is the Economy Growing?

The last and the most important problem is to find out whether the economy is growing through time or is it stagnant. If the economy is stagnant at any point inside the production possibility curve, it has to be moved on to the production possibility curve PP whereby the economy now produces larger quantities of consumer goods and capital goods. Economic growth takes place through a higher rate of capital formation which consists of replacing existing capital goods with new and more productive ones by adopting more efficient production techniques or through innovations.

All of these economy problems will be our societies often causes to anyone feels need to solve problems in order to achieve our societies can have enough resources to satisfy our every day living.

● The Consumer Problem

Consumer theory is concerned with how a rational consumer would make consumption decisions. What makes this problem worthy of separate study, apart from the general problem of choice theory, is its particular structure that allows us to derive economically meaningful results. The structure arises because the consumer's choice sets are assumed to be defined by certain prices and the consumer's income or wealth. The consumer's problem is to choose that is most preferred or, equivalently, that has the greatest utility.

The assumption of perfect information is built deeply into the formulation of this choice problem, just as it is in the underlying choice theory. Some alternative models treat the consumer as rational but uncertain about the products, for example how a particular food will taste or a how well a cleaning product will perform. Some goods may be experience goods which the consumer can best learn about by trying ("experiencing") the good. In that case, the consumer might want to buy some now and decide later whether to buy more. That situation would need a different formulation. Similarly, if the agent thinks that high price goods are more likely to perform in a satisfactory way, that, too, would suggest quite a different formulation. Agents are price-takers. The agent takes prices p as known, fixed and exogenous. This assumption excludes things like searching for better prices or bargaining for a discount.

Hence , it seems that economic problems and consumer problems are similar, I feel that it is possible , economists can attempt to apply any economic theories to solve some consumer problems in some situations. They can find the accurate solutions when they can apply the suitable economic theories to solve the suitable consumer or economic problems in our societies. I shall indicate that how economists can apply the suitable economic theories to attempt to solve some consumer problems in our societies as below:

Demand And Supply Theory Solves Consumer Problems

What is economy rule predict consumer behaviour? Why and How does economist can apply economy rule to predict consumer behaviours? I shall explain the reasons as below:

Why does economic principle be the best to predict consumer behaviour. It may include these two reasons: The first focuses on the substantive domain of study, in this interpretation , economics is a social science devoted to understanding how the economy works. The second definition focuses on methods: economics is a way of doing social science, using particular tools. In this interpretation the discipline is associated with formal modelling and statistical analysis rather than particular hypotheses or theories about the economy. Therefore, economic methods can be applied to many other areas besides the economy, everything from decisions within the family to questions about political institutions.

● Demand and supply principle predict public transport tool passenger behaviour

Economists need to use the right economic ideas to predict consumer behaviour. So, Misuse the wrong economy ideas to predict consumer behaviours. It will do more wrong judgement to evaluate or predict why and how and when the country's consumer behaviours will change. It is every economist needs to consider issue. For example, the economy idea application of economic supply-demand principles to public transport. Different fares would give commuters with more-flexible hours the incentive to avoid peak travel times. They would allow passenger traffic to spread out over time, reducing the pressure on the public transport system when enabling even larger total passenger flow. IT aims to reduce traffic congestion, increased public-transport use, reduced car-bon emissions and cause air pollution and generated considerable revenue for the country's transport system. So, if the country can apply supply and demand economic principle to attempt to predict how many passengers number needs to catch transport tools to go to work or go to school or other activities. Then, it can predict how many bus, ferry, taxi, train, underground train, tram etc. different public transport tools to satisfy future public transport passengers' needs in society. So, this demand and supply principle is the comparative best rule to predict any kinds of public transport passengers' road needs, when they need to either go to school, go to office, go to leisure or shopping etc. different kinds of activities. So, applying the demand and supply principle to predict road and sea public transport passengers can help the country to reduce air pollution when they feel that they can find any public transport tools to catch any time conveniently , then it can encourage them to reduce car purchase desire. When many people choose to catch public transport tools, then it will reduce many cars number on the road. Then, air pollution will reduce as well as any public transport tools' income will also increase as well as traffic jam will also reduce. When the country can evaluate how many people choose to catch bus or taxi or ferry or train or underground train, or tram or train etc. different kinds of public transport tools, then the country can predict the more accurate public transport tools number to every kind of public transport tool to satisfy their journey needs. e.g. whether underground train or train or tram need to decrease or increase the frequent times or number to catch the volume of passenger in busy or non-busy time; or whether bus company has need to increase how much buses to catch the city location passengers when they are living in the city. Moreover, supply and demand principle can help any public transport tools to explain why their passengers number reduces in the year, it may due to fare charge is unreasonable, feeling uncomfortable to sit on the seat or air condition is poor in the transport tool environment, or there are no more seats because many there are much time is full passenger and no seat vacancy to provide to them to sit . So, supply and demand principle can help any kinds of public transport tools to find whether which is (are) the factor(S) can influence the current or last year passengers number reduce. Then, they can concentrate on improving their weaknesses to raise their service quality . So, supply and demand principle can also help they to evaluate whether what their weakness are in order to improve to increase passengers number. They can do questionnaires to enquiry their passengers' response to evaluate whether which areas of services that they feel unsatisfactory. So, the different kinds of service satisfactory feeling to the passengers number data will be the main source to help the kind of public transport tool to analyse and conclude the results more accurate, then they can make the more accurate judgement to improve the of service.

For example, the questionnaires indicate that the many passengers feel the bus fare is reasonable, but many passengers feel they can not find any seats to sit easily. So, it implies that the bus firm ought buy more buses or enlarges bus size and increases more seats in the enlarged buses. Then, it does not reduce its fare but it needs to find solutions to let passengers can find seats to sit in every bus more easily. But, if the questionnaires indicate that there are many passengers feel its fare is higher or unreasonable to compare other kinds of public transportation tools. Hence, it can avoid to spend more expenditure to increase bus number to the city, if the city has many passengers , they still choose bus to catch, but they feel its fare is too higher to compare other kinds of public transport tool. Then, it only needs to reduce its fare , it ought help it to increase passengers number. Hence, demand and supply principle is the most suitable economic method to evaluate any kinds of public transport system passenger needs in any country nowadays.

● Supply and demand and price elasticities principle predict oil energy user behaviour

The another case is that demand and supply principle can predict oil buyer behaviour to find whether what factors can cause the oil buyer individual need reduces. For example , a rise in production costs increases market prices and reduces quantities demanded and supplied. Or when, energy cost rise, utility bills increases and households fid extra ways of saving heating and electricity. But, others are nor. For example, whether a tax is imposed on the producers or consumer of a commodity, say oil has nothing to do with who ends up paying for it. The tax might be administered on oil companies, but it might be consumers who really pay for it through higher prices at the pump. Or the extra cost might be imposed on consumers in the form of a sale tax, but the oil companies might be forces to absorb it through lower prices. It all depends on the " price elasticities" of demand and supply. With the addition of extra assumption, this model also generates rather strong implications about how well markets work. In particular, a competitive market economy is efficient in the sense that it is impossible to improve one person's well-being without reducing somebody.

● Demand and supply principle can misuse to predict consumer behaviour when the two firms participate advertisement to promote their products in the same time

Why can demand and supply principle misuse to predict consumer behaviour when the two firms participate advertisement to promote their products in the same time ? I shall explain as below: Assume that two competing firms must decide whether to have a big advertising budget. Advertising would allow one firm to steal some of the other's customers. But when they both advertise, the effects on customer demand cancel out. The firms end up having spent money needlessly.

We might expect that neither firm would choose to spend much on advertising, but the model shows that this logic is off base. When the firms make their choices independently and they care only about their own profits, each one has an incentive to advertise, regardless of what the other firm does. When the other firm does not advertise, you can steal customers from it if you do advertise, when the other firm does advertise, you have to advertise to prevent loss of customers. So, these two firms end up in a bad equilibrium in which both have to waste resources. This market can not apply demand and supply principle to predict consumer behaviours because they depends advertisement to promote their products. If these two firms advertise their products in the same time. Then , it is not possible that if one firm increases it price and it will cause its customer number loss, due to its advertise can help it to attract customers to consider its product from television or radio or newspapers or magazine promotion channels. So, I suppose that these two firms decide to increase their price, when they advertise their products to let customers to know in the same time. They will not lose their customers or reduce their customers easily. Because their customers can be persuaded to choose to buy their products to compare other similar products in preference. So, their increasing price will not influence their customers number lose easily. It explains that demand and supply principle is not right to this case, so demand and supply principle can misuse to help them to predict consumer behaviours when they advertise their products in the same time. Also, demand and supply principle is not suitable to them to predict consumer behaviours when they advertise their products in the same time. They will do wrong prediction to their consumers purchase desire when they advertise their products in the same time.

ON conclusion, using these demand and supply and price elasticity techniques, economists derive specific prediction for how consumers choose which products to buy, how households save, how firms invest, how workers search for jobs, as well as for how these actions depend on the particulars. They can help them to predict job and consumption behaviours more accurate, it depends on whether the situation is right, such as both competition firms participate to advertise their products in the same time case, it is not right to apply above economic principle to predict consumer behaviours. They will get wrong prediction when they apply this principle to predict consumer behaviours.

However, demand and supply principle can predict below any one of these cases. I shall indicate as below:

The problem of need-based scholarships: Most systems for providing college scholarships are based on some definition of financial needs, with scholarships generally being given only to those students who must need financial help in order to attend school.

Is need, rather than academic ability, the best basic on which to choose those students who are to be encouraged to attend college? Which way of choosing who gets aids is the more just? Which is the more efficient ? Is the overall educational level of society increased more by giving financial aid to bright students or to needy students? Presumably the aid offers more leverage to needy students, since they all need the money in order to attend college, whereas, many of the bright students would attend college in any case. But is a smaller number of bright students the more important addition?

So, the school can apply demand and supply principle to predict whether how many parents feel need financial assistance and evaluate how much financial amount is the right to borrow. It aims to calculate how many parents feel real financial need and how much to lend to them in order to let these students to get the most fair financial assistance.

Assuming the school wish to use need as a basis, how does the school determines " financial need"?

Is need a function or parents' income? What, then , does the school about children of wealthy parents who are living independently of them and get no aid from parents? Should they be punished for their parents' wealth? But if they are given aid, won't all students, in order to get aid, claim to be independent of their parents?

Is need solely a matter of family income, or should not the school takes a family's financial obligations into account? Does not it make more sense to give aid to someone whose parents must put night more children through school than to someone from a family of five or one only with the same income? But in a possible parallel situations, should a family that carries mortgages on one or two large homes get preference simply because they do not have much money left to spend on college? Does doing this reward ? Is there a difference between the case of night children and the case of the large mortgage? How should parents who are not married , but are living together and supporting their children jointly be counted? Most parents are supporter to their children , although they are married in possible.

So, the school needs to gather all these data to evaluate how many parents are not married or married or living with their children together, how much salary they earn as well as every family has how much children as well as whether they have mortgage for their houses. So, these number will be the financial education assistance demanders, but it does not represent their real financial needs. It is possible that someone does not feel any financial need, although their children apply financial assistance to your school. Then , your school needs to evaluate whether how much financial assistance can lend to every real financial need student family. It can not exceed your final financial expenditure budget (supply) , when your financial expenditure is not enough. SO, demand and supply principle can be applied to research this school real family financial demand to lend to the real financial need families and evaluate whether the reasonable financial amount to lend to every child family to study in your school.

● Supply and demand principle applies to immigration to decide wage case

A fascinating and important example of supply and demand, full of complexities, is the role of immigration in determining wages. If you ask people , they are likely to tell you that immigration into California or Florida US, surely lowers the wages of people in those regions. It is just supply and demand analysis of immigration. According to this analysis, of these to these two regions in US. Immigration in to a region shifts the supply curve for labor to the right and pushes down wages. Why has it relationship between immigration to US these two regions immigrant number and wage?

Careful economic studies cast doubt on this simple proposition, however, a recent survey of the evidence concludes:

The effect of immigration on the labor market outcomes of natives is small in US. There is no evidence of economically significant reductions in native employment. Most analysis, finds that a 10 percent increase in the fraction of immigrants in the population reduced native wages by a most 1%.

How can we explain the small impact of immigration on wages? The main mistake is to forget how mobile the American population is and that the impact of immigration on wages, we must examine the effect of new immigrants when the strength of the local economy and the number of native-born residents in a city are unchanged, that is , when these other things are held constant. Unless you exclude the effects other changing variables, you can not accurately predict the impact of immigration. The same principle holds in doing a supply0and demand analysis of any market. As much as possible, when you are examining the impact of a supply or demand shift, you must try to keep all other things constant.

● Rationing by prices

By determining the equilibrium prices and quantities of all inputs and outputs, the market allocated or rations out the scare goods of the society among the possible uses. Who does the rationing? A planning board? Congress or the president? BO, the marketplace, through the interaction of supply and demand, doe the rationing. This is rationing by the purse.

What foods are produces? This is answered by the signals of the market price. High oil prices stimulates oil production, whereas low food prices drive resources out of agriculture. Those who have the most dollars votes have the greatest influences on what goods are produced. All of these considers how demand and supply to the market.

For whom are goods produces? The power of the pursue indicates the distribution of income and consumption. Those with higher incomes end up with larger houses, more clothing, and linger vacations. When the most urgently felt needs get fulfilled through the demand curve.

Even, the how question is decided by supply and demand. When corn prices are low, it is not profitable for farmers to use expensive tractors and irrigation systems, and only the best land is cultivated. When oil prices are high, oil companies drill in deep offshore waters and employ novel seismic techniques to find oil.

IN sum , any thing needs through demands, interact with costs of goods, as reflected in supplies in our economic world. Hence, demand and supply theory ought be the most accurate method to help any businesses or governments to predict their shareholders behaviours when they will change as well as how and how their behaviours change.

Consumer choice theory solves consumer problems

What is 'consumer choice theory'?

'Consumer choice theory' is a hypothesis about why people buy things. Put simply, it says that you choose to buy the things that give you the greatest satisfaction, while keeping within your budget. At the heart of this theory are three assumptions about human nature.[1]

The first assumption is that when you shop, you choose to buy things based on calculated decisions about what will make you happiest. In economics language, this is known as utility maximisation (Economists really like to put quite simple concepts into long complicated terms.)

Secondly, the theory assumes that no matter how much you shop, you will never be completely satisfied. In other words, you will always be happier consuming a little bit more. This is known as the principle of non-satiation. Thirdly, even though you always get more happiness from more consumption, the amount of pleasure you get from each good decreases with the more you consume. So if you eat two ice creams rather than one, you get more overall pleasure, but the second ice-cream won't be as satisfying as the first. This is known as decreasing marginal utility.

Consumer choice theory has influenced everything from government policy to corporate advertising to academia. But the theory has been criticized for not being the most accurate description of how people actually make choices. A whole new branch of economics, called 'behavioral economics', has emerged essentially to use findings from psychology to disprove the assumptions behind consumer choice theory. This has also led others to argue that consumer choice theory is less about describing how we do actually behave, and is more about describing how people should behave.[3] In other words, by portraying people as self-interested shopaholics, economists are saying that is it okay and natural for us to be avid consumers.

● Consumer choice theory can be applied to solve consumer problems during the country can have economic growth , the reasons may include as below:

The scenario leading to inflation starts with poor growth. Forget about everything that comes next and focus on that most important factor. Because it happens that the scenario leading to a budget crisis also starts with poor growth, and the scenario leading to a long-term unemployment crisis starts with poor growth, and a scenario leading to a better-the-neighbor trade crisis starts with poor growth, and so on. So a very important question is: what can be done to improve the prospects for economic growth? In particular, what is the right countercyclical approach to take to best situate the economy for future growth? I shall indicate during US, America's economy growth occurs, then economists can attempt to apply customer choice theory to solve US itself country's consumer problems more easier.

In no small part, the question comes down to interpretations of charts like the one at right. On the one hand, long and deep downturns seem to have almost no effect on the long-term rate of growth. On the other hand, in the long run we're all dead, and those who live during an extended period of economic weakness suffer for it. Meanwhile, it's also difficult to see where high debt levels influence the long-run rate of growth, at least where this chart is concerned.

During to the medium-term growth stage, is the bigger threat to American growth rates a market revolt against American debt levels? Or is it structural unemployment stemming from the slow, jobless recovery? Or is the cyclical shortfall in public investment? Or something else entirely? Of course, there's no real reason one has to choose a problem to address at the expense of others. More aggressive monetary expansion could make the finding of a solution to all these problems easier, but the Fed is unwilling to oblige me on this score. It may well be concerned that lack of fiscal discipline will lead to increasing inflation expectations, making its job harder (but then fiscal problems are trace able to growth). If that is the worry, however, one has to ask why the Congress has been unable to strike a deal for $20 billion in stimulus this year for $80 billion in fiscal tightening in a year or two (fill in whatever amounts you wish). But the outlook for the American economy vis-a-vis any number of potential crises will hinge on growth, and growth will hinge on the ability of private business to exploit promising opportunities as they arise. And the question is: what's likely to hurt that ability most? High interest rates? Lack of consumer demand? A shortage of adequately prepared workers? Right now firms appear to be most worried about demand shortfalls. So how much can you boost demand without making the primary fear high interest rates? A lot, if the expansion is on the monetary side.

● How to supply consumer choice theory to predict Consumer Behavior Marketing at Apple Computer

During US economy growth, Apply computer applies consumer choice theory to solve its computer buyers' choice problems among different kinds of brand computer competitors. Have you ever wondered why Apple is so successful? They were not the first company to invent the personal computer, portable music device, the tablet, the smartphone, software to download music, or the set-top box to name a few. Apple has amassed a brand loyal following like no other brand backed by significant sales, market share, and profitability. So, how does Apple do it? What's the secret behind their success?

Marketing using consumer behavior insight is how Apple succeeds. Even though Steve Jobs and Apple, did not use consumer research in the initial development of most products, consumer behavior plays a huge role in their marketing and ultimately the success of the company. Once a consumer purchases a product or downloads iTunes Apple has access to data the company leverages. Apple uses this information to gain significant insight into the consumer and what drives purchase behavior.

Consumer behavior marketing is an essential ingredient in the current business climate. The companies that apply this type of marketing well have a distinct competitive advantage that distances them from their rivals. Consumer behavior research is the primary driver at the core of any good strategy. Research provides actionable insight and ensures business success. If you answer no to the following questions, this post is for you?

·Are you applying consumer behavior marketing currently?

·Have you conducted consumer behavior research within the last two years?

·Do you have consumer behavior marketing in your marketing plan with well-defined marketing strategies and tactics?

·Are you achieving the maximum results for your organization?

Every business has a target audience and consumer behavior marketing provides the fundamental methods for understanding your target. Consumer behavior research provides the underlying element that drives quality strategies and ensures business results.

"Marketing is understanding your buyers really, really well. Then creating valuable products, services, and information especially for them to help solve their problems."

The organizations that have an intimate understanding of their target audience possess a competitive advantage over those that do not. Establishing a one-to-one relationship and thorough knowledge of your target audience is a core responsibility for business in the 21st century and beyond. Regardless if you are B2B, B2C, B2G or a hybrid organization you have a target audience. The information in this post can be applied to any business type. This post focuses on Apple (B2C) employing consumer behavior marketing as a critical ingredient for their success.

Hence, Apply computer shops have several computer teachers to teach any visitors how to use its laptops, hen they enquire its any computer salespeople. Due to its salespeople had been trained to learn how to use the different kinds of laptops. So, anyone enquires them, they can answer their enquires concern any computer questions immediately. Then, they will feel Apple laptops are the first choice to compare other kinds of laptops brands. It is one salespeople answering strategies to persuade any Apple computer visitors to feel its any laptops are the first or preference choice to compare its competitors in this computer market, so customer choice economic theory is the most suitable strategy to solve Apple computer's customer individual purchase decision problem.

Microeconomics Models and Theories solve customer problems

Microeconomics is concerned with the economic decisions and actions of individuals and firms. Within the broad church of microeconomics, there are different theories that certain assumptions and expectations of economic behaviour. The most important theory is neo-classical theory, which places emphasis on free-markets and the assumption individuals are rational and seek to maximise utility. However, there are many critiques of the neo-classical model, arguing economics is more complex with issues of market failure and irrational behaviour.

Pre-classical microeconomic theory

Before, Adam Smith, economics was more disparate with no commanding overall theory. Philosophers like Aristotle and Plato made references to issues in economics such as division of labour. The dominant ideas, pre-classical economics, were based on theories of mercantilism – the idea a nation should try to accumulate gold.

Classical microeconomic theory

Classical microeconomic theory was developed by Adam Smith (Wealth of Nations, 1776) and later economists, such as David Ricardo The essential aspect of classical microeconomic theory include:

Adam Smith mentioned the 'invisible hand of the market.' He noted how when people act out of self-interest, markets tend to provide goods and services which are demanded by the population. It needed no central price setting, but market forces responded to changes in demand and supply, e.g. a shortage pushes up the price and causes demand to fall.

Smith also investigated topics such as the division of labour, specialisation and economies of scale. The early classical economists emphasised the importance of costs to firms and consumers.

Utility maximisation

An important development of classical economics towards the end of the nineteenth century is the concept of utility maximisation. The concept of utility was developed by philosophers/economists – Jeremy Bentham and John Stuart Mill. In microeconomic theory, it was believed a consumer will buy goods depending on the marginal utility (satisfaction) they get from the good. This theory assumes consumers are rational and seeking to maximise the satisfaction they get.

Neo-classical theory

Neo-classical theory is a modern re-interpretation of classical economics of the nineteenth century. Neo-classical theory places importance on markets, but developed new ideas, especially regarding utility and rational choice theory. Elements of neo-classical theory.

1. Market distribution of goods and services.

2.R ational choice theory. This is the idea individuals hold rational preferences and make rational choices; seeking to maximise their outcomes – be it profit, wages, consumption or investment.

3. People act independently and make use of available information.

4. Marginalism. In neo-classical economics, more emphasis was placed on concepts of marginal utility and marginal cost. We make choices depending on satisfaction we get from one extra unit of a good.

Economists such as Carl Menger, William Stanley Jevons and Marie-Esprit-Léon Walras. and Alfred Marshall developed ideas such as diminishing marginal utility. Many of these neo-classical economic theories were brought together in Alfred Marshall's very influential textbook, Principles of Economics. (1890)

·Note there is some blurring between classical economics and neo-classical economics.

·Neo-classical economics has also come to mean 'orthodox economic theory. To a large extent, it has incorporated new developments in microeconomics, such as theories of market failure, market structure and econometrics.

Theories of Market failure

Neo-classical economics has become associated with a belief in the efficiency of markets. However, microeconomic theory has also incorporated the criticisms and limitations of free-markets.

·Monopoly. Adam Smith was well aware of the problem of monopolies and how firms could use their market power to set excessive prices.

·Imperfect competition. In the 1930s, Joan Robinson developed a model of imperfect competition, an awareness many markets were somewhere between monopoly and perfect competition often assumed in neo-classical economics.

·Externalities. Developed by Arthur C.Pigou in The Economics of Welfare (1920) this is the awareness production and consumption decisions can have harmful (or positive) effects on third parties. Therefore, a free market can lead to overconsumption of demerit goods and negative externalities.

·Game theory. An awareness, decisions are not linear or simple, but the interdependence of agents influences what we decide to do.

Behavioural economics

The most important trend in recent decades in economics is the greater emphasis placed on aspects of behavioural economics, which uses many insights from related fields such as psychology.

·Disputes rational choice theory. The essential element of behavioural economics is that it argues individual agents are often not rational and often do not seek to maximise utility.

·Behavioural economics examines how agents can be influenced by biases, and make decisions not predicted by neo-classical economic theory. Behavioural economics can explain the irrational exuberance of booms and busts.

Econometrics

In the post-war period, economics became increasingly mathematical with economists attempting to use mathematics to explain models and theories. Econometrics looks at economic data and seeks to extract simple relationships. The basic tool is the linear regression models and can be used to try and predict consumer spending and demand for labour.

Heterodox models of microeconomics

Heterodox models differ substantially from microeconomic foundations of neo-classical economics. Schools of thought include

Marxist economic theory

Karl Marx developed an alternative perspective on economics. He focused on the surplus value created under the capitalist economic system. To Marx, the invisible hand of the market would be better described as the invisible hand of capitalist exploitation of workers. Marx claimed workers did receive their full labour value but were compensated for their necessary labour only – enabling capitalists to profit from the surplus.

Institutional economics. The role of society and institutions in shaping economic behaviour. For example, Thomas Veblen looked at theories of 'conspicuous consumption' and noted how the desire for social status could drive much economic theory. Institutional economics could be seen as a forerunner for later behavioural economics.

Environmental economics Argues traditional economics wrongly places value on increasing output. The most important thing is creating a sustainable environment which maximises living standards. So, manufacturers need to consider how to manufacture their products , but pollution can not be raised as the same time, because human will face to raise cost of living and living experiences to be poor , even food shortage, water pollution , air pollution , death rate raises when technological productivities brings pollution to our natural environment. Hence, environmental economoic theory is the most suitable to solve manufacturers' pollution problem.

Buddhist economics/non-profit goals. Like environmental economics, this questions the assumption higher incomes and higher output are desirable. The theory of hedonistic relativism suggests higher incomes do nothing to increase happiness levels, and traditional economics can encourage society to pursue materialistic goals which actually create more problems of stress, conflict and environmental degradation.

Some of the basic models you might find in A-Level economics :

·Price Discrimination
·Perfect competition
·Price Mechanism
·Monopoly
·Oligopoly and kinked demand curve
·Game Theory Pricing strategies
·Market failure
·Behavioural economics

ON conclusion, any macro economy theories can be applied to find the most reasonable methods to solve any customer problems in societies by economists as above. So, I believe that any economic and customer and social problems can be solved by economic theories in our society.

Demand and supply theory solves social problems

Over the past 20 years, many researchers believe to apply behavioral economic macroeconomic models which can predict market behavioral change. The reasons are based on assumptions of optimizing behavior in many cases have difficulty accounting for key real-world observations.

Hence, researchers have used behavioral economics assumptions with the aim of making their model predicting better fit the data. The reason for behavioral economics results into macroeconomics will be more accurate to predict market behavioral change in macro-economy view point, such as economic fluctuation prediction, the consumption, formation of expectations and determination of wages and employment how to aggregation supply and the possibility of consumer individual demand product or service number prediction more accurately.

● How to apply behavioral economy (demand and supply) theory to predict marketing behavioral changes more accurate?

Anyway, economists aim to develop models of human behavior and interactions in market in order to build useful models. Economists make simplifying assumptions to analyze why the market will be changed by consumer individual consumption behavior changing.

Why do I assume consumers are as economic man ? In behavioral economy view point, how the perception of the economic man's behavior (including consumer choices) of economic models with the development of economics as a science. Economists explain the concept of economics as a science. It is the concept of consumer as an economic man, the essence and complexity of consumer behavior.

The consumer and consumer purchasing behavior are an important area of interest of many scientific disciplines. The process of economic decision making as well as consumption choices are connected with wider human activities. The terms of both consumer individual attitudes and group social behavior will influence group social behavior will influence consumer individual final consumption decision in every consumption choice process. Thus, behavioral economy method can predict consumer behavioral changing, it can apply these sciences to research, includes sociology, psychology, anthropology, operational research, decision theory etc. different literature research aspects. I assume that businessmen can apply behavioral economy method to predict market changing behaviors successfully if they own behavioral economy knowledge.

In this part, I shall concentrate on explain how the perception of the economic man's behavior (including consumer choice) is applied to predict market behaviors. After explaining the concept of consumer as an economic man, the nature and complexity of consumer behavior are discussed to below different industries' marketing behavioral changing every case studies in US or UK countries.

Why is consumer as an economic man? IN behavioral economy view point, the concept of answer is one of the fundamental concepts in economics because the consumer is the case market participant along with the producer. In general, lecturers define the consumer in various ways, but in behavioral economy view point, consumers mean economy man. Because who will compare cost and benefit to any product or service to decide to choose to buy the product or consume the service. Consumers are as "economic man", who will make own subjective preferences (tastes), habits and traditions and existing objective constraints (i.e. disposal income) market prices of products and services in order to satisfy whose needs to a maximum degree and in the most rational way.

Thus, economic man means consumers need to make psychological mind to decide whether who either prefer to buy this product or another product or prefer to consume this service or another service more suitable. Thus, any markets or industries need have themselves benefits and consumers must need to evaluate whether the product or service has more benefits to compare other products or services in the consumption market to satisfy whose needs. It means that if the product or service has more benefits to compare other similar products or services. Then the product or service will persuade many consumers to choose to but the product or consume the service.

Consequently, in first part, I shall indicate how to apply behavioral economy theory : economic man psychological method, benefits and costs benefits method, how to predict these US and UK enterprises marketing behavioral changing more accurate.

In the second part, I shall apply micro employee behavioral economy concept to explain how to solve these US and UK inter-organizational management challenge.

I believe that behavioral economy method can be applied to research organizational employee behaviors change, e.g. how any why the employee chooses to do this action in whose organization. Moreover, behavioral economy method can be applied to consumption market to predict how any why the consumer choose to buy the product or consume the service. So, any consumers and employees personal psychology and external environment economic factor will influence how to choose to do decision in any organizations or consumption environment.

Bibliography

Bandiera, O., I. Barankay, and I. Rasul (2005). Social preferences and the response to incentives: Evidence from personal data. The quarterly journal of economics 120 (3), 917-969.

Exadaktylos, F., A.M. Espin and P. Branas-Garza (2013). Experimental subjects are not different. Scientific reports 3, 1213.

Lazear, E.P. (1979). Why is there mandatory retirement? Journal of political economy 87(6), 1261-1284.

● Behavioral economic method (demand and supply theory) predicts stable basic income consumer individual spending behavior

Can apply behavioral economic method to predict that the consequences of a stable basic income consumer's consumption behavior? It may be significantly different than the ones are predicted by the standard economic model if more realistic assumptions of human consumption behavioral prediction success.

Behavioral economic method assumes that consumer will compare whether whose benefits are more than costs after they buy the product or consume the service. I assume the consumer is only the who have stable basic income source consumer target. This stable basic income target consumers who will evaluate or feel they will earn more benefits than costs to every product in their consumption process, after they will make final decision to choose to buy the product to use or consume the service. Otherwise, if they feel they won't earn more benefits after they buy the product or consume the service in the consumption process. Then, they won't choose to buy the product to use or consume the service. In behavioral economic view point, it indicates their consumption behaviors are depend on comparing the product or the service whether it can satisfy their desire benefits and their desire benefits to the product or service must be more than their consumption cost.

There are four points to apply behavioral economic method to predict each stable basic income individual income spending. They include: motivation, conspicuous consumption, social preferences and crowding theory.

Each stable basic income consumer individual spending amount will be different and it is represent that every high stable basic income consumer must decide to consume any high cost services or buy high cost products to use. Although some economic teachers assume general high income people will accept to spend more expenditures for enjoyment or buy high cost of products to satisfy basic high level necessary expenditures. But, applying behavioral economic analysis, it is not absolute true, some low income people also accept to spend more to buy high cost of products or increasing spending expenditures for enjoyment for their basic necessary expenditures.

The field of behavioral economic can be fined as a combination of economics and psychology that tries to capture human behavior in a more realistic. Understanding each consumer individual consumption behavior, we need to know how who does each decision to influence each consumption choice. Consequently, analysis reaches the conclusion. Every high or low level stable basic income consumer individual behavioral consumption that the microeconomic consequences of a stable basic income of individual consumer target consumption group could be efficiency enhancing, but at the same time incentives about positional concerns could lead to wasteful and inefficient spending to the stable low basic income consumer target group.

● How to apply demand and supply theory to contribute to the stable basic income target consumer group's consumption prediction?

What is basic income mean? A basic income is an income paid by a political community to all its members on an individual basis, without means test or work requirement. How to apply behavioral economic method to contribute to the basic income consumption prediction?

I assume high income tax is charged to one high income tax payee , it will influence the high income tax payee individual consumption desires to be fallen, also extrinsic incentives will effort and intrinsic motivation and how the labor market change these variables under and big changes predicting, how income security changes social consumption preferences, e.g. how a big change affects the overall level of status -seeking behavior and this effect with income inequality to influence consumer individual consumption attitude or habit.

How can behavioral economic methods predict consumer's consumption decision, in special the stable basic income consumer target group? In any consumption decisions are involving risk and uncertainty, the standard economic model usually assumes that decisions are based on final condition, regardless of the changes are caused by the results of a consumer's decision.

An alterative mode of how consumers make decision and judgement under risk and uncertainty. This situation is often occurred in consumption market.

In behavioral economic view point, it explains how consumer's consumption, however, which excludes the stable basic income earn factor can influence the stable basic income earn target consumer group decides to make final consumption decision to compare to the non-stable basic income earn target consumer group. The reasons include as below:

(1) Consumers evaluate decisions over gains and losses with respect to some natural reference point, when they feel need to consume, which is assumed to be judgement about a sequence of outcomes are based on changes in wealth, rather than whether how much absolute basic income earn to influence whose consumption desires.

(2) Thus, behavioral economic theory assumes the consumer is the low level of income group in society, but when who feels that he is still gains more than losses when who decides to buy the expensive product or consumes the expensive service. Then, the low level of income consumer who will accept to buy the expensive product or consume the service easily. Due to whose gains feeling is more than losses feeling, when who buys the product or consumes the service.

(3) Behavioral economic theory also assumes the taxpayer will pay high income tax in this year. The, even the high income taxpayer can earn high basic income, but due to whom needs to pay high income tax in this year. Then, he/she will reduce much spending, even he/she reduces spending on cheap products or cheap service consumption for enjoyment. This is the taxpayer's economic decision to influence whose consumption behavior, due to the high income tax expenditure factor influences whose consumption behavior to change to be reduced spending expenditures in this year.

How to apply behavioral economic method to predict labor market changing behavior?

Instead of applying behavioral economic method to predict every consumer individual consumption effort. Behavioral economic method can be also be applied to predict every country's labor market changing behavior. Particularly, how salary clerical workers or low wage labor workers should move from one type of job to another based on these factors. They include as below:

Their intrinsic motivation and how their levels of effort would change after this movement, investigates the effects of income security on social preferences in labor market changing behavior, and how cooperation in social contribution is affected when income security is guaranteed, how to predict the role of positional externalities on conspicuous consumption and how would change the incentive to influence consumption. So, it seems that general labor market job changing behaviors will not influenced by external economic environment better or worse changing factor, or salary changing factor etc. different environmental condition changing factors influence to employees' job changing. Generally, employee's job changing behavior is more influenced to persuade who changes job by himself/herself intrinsic motivation negative emotion influence mainly.

How to apply motivation crowding theory to predict labor productivity? One of the main challenges of economic theory is to find what are the optimal incentives that increase productivity of labors. The standing point is usually extrinsic incentive be it is form of monetary compensations for high effort or fine for low effort.

It is a kind method of reward or punishment to increase or decrease number of productivity to every labor. But it can only raise short term number of productivity in possible and it can not guarantee high quality of productivity. So if one employer wants a labor to do more of an activity or with a higher quality, consider paying the labor for working hard on punishing whom if for providing a low level effort.

This idea is that people do not like to work, and therefore they used some sort of compensation for doing a specific activity, and that the more they are paid the harder, they will work. So, payment better compensation is only beneficial to encourage labors to do one specific task or activity in short term. This method can not be suitable to rise long term beneficial productivity and high level quality of production or excellent performance in long term and it can only keep in short term raising productivity and high level quality of production or excellent performance benefits.

Consider paying the labor for working hard on punishing whom if for providing a low level effort. This idea is that people do not like to work, and therefore they used some sort of compensation for doing a specific activity, and that the more they are paid the harder they will work. So, payment better compensation is only beneficial to encourage labors to do one specific task or activity in short term. This method can not be suitable to raise long them beneficial productivity and high quality of products.

However, economists would argue that, is a labor has high intrinsic motivative to perform a task, who will provide a high level of effort without compensation by himself/herself but an even higher level of effort of whom is compensated. If a labor does not have any intrinsic motivation to perform a task or an activity, who will provide no effort or a low effort of whom.

There is no compensation, but who will increase this level of effort of an extrinsic incentive is implemented.

Hence, in behavioral economic view point, the labor individual high level effort is a main psychological factor to influence whose productivity to be raised or the qualities of products to be raised, when the products are manufactured by the high level effort labor. It means that high compensation is not the good method to encourage labor productivity or raise quality. Otherwise, how to influence the one low level of effort of labor to change to be one high level of effort labor. It is the best psychological method to influence the labor to raise productivity and quality and service performance to any products or services in manufacturing process or service process for any organizations in long term beneficial possible.

● How can apply demand and supply theory raises basic stable income consumer consumption desire

Economists aim to develop models of human behavior and interactions in consumption markets. But consumers behave in complex ways, such as how to predict consumers to make rational decisions in consumption processes. Moreover, self-consumption control and motivation can vary significantly across different individual consumer.

In order to build useful consumption prediction models, economists make simplifying assumptions, aims to predict how to raise stable basic income consumer target group consumption more success. However, behavioral economy method is one kind of accurate consumption prediction method. It can be applied to predict economic decision-making to every consumer consumption choice more accurate raising whose consumption desire?

I shall indicate how to apply different behavioral economy methods (demand and supply theory) to raise stable basic stable income target consumer group consumption desire in these different consumption situation (consumption environment) aspects as below:

1. Stable basic stable income consumer group consumption great or small amount desire

The consumption of products and services is a fundamental part of consumer's welfare. Basically, every one who has stable basic stable income, who will like to consume any products and services. Even, consumption great or small amount desire won't be depended on whether the person whose income is more or less. It means low income level of people will still like to consume great amount to buy expensive products or consume expensive services, because consumption is human's part of life and basic needs.

This stable basic income people will like to consume, because they have stable income source when they do not worry about unemployment occurrence to cause them have no enough money to support their life. Otherwise, non-stable basic stable income people won't like to consume because they feel they have no stable basic income source to support their life and they will worry about unemployment occurrence any time. Hence, stable basic income people will have more consumption desire to compare non-stable basic stable income people in any countries usually. Behavioral economic method indicates they feel their economic benefits will be loss if they planned to buy any products or consume any services easily. So, they prefer to save money in bank more than consumption.

1. Demand systems and micro-economic factor influence basic income people consumption attitude

Why stable basic income people will like to consume? Because who have more demand, a demand system shows the level of consumer demand for different products and services: e.g. one basic stable income person may refer to the demand for clothes, another the demand for food etc.

How the demand for that particular product varies with the prices and demographic factor will influence who to accept consumption. Such as stable basic income people who will not consider to decide to buy the cloth to wear or the food to eat if who feel the cloth or food price is even more expensive to compare other kind of cloth or food.

Otherwise, non-stable basic income people who will consider to decide to buy the cloth to wear or the food to eat if they feel that they still have enough cloths to wear or enough food to eat at homes , even these food or cloth price are less expensive to compare others. Because they feel they lack stable income effort to support them to consume. Hence, basic stable income factor can influence the consumer's consumption decision.

2. Life-cycle advertisement method can influence consumer individual consumption behaviors to be increased

Consumer behavior makes strong assumptions about the informational and computational bases of consumer behavior. Generally, consumer behavior is reasonably characterized as the maximization of expected lifetime utility subject to budget constraint and conditional on the available information.

Generally, consumers prefer to buy any discounted products or it is reasonable that consumers accept to buy many attractions to persuade them to buy any kinds of bargain discount products. Hence, low bargain discount product is one good behavioral economic principle to encourage or persuade or attract any consumers to increase consumption.

What is behavioral life-cycle model? This model explains consumer behavior can be persuaded to buy any discounted products by advertisement, e.g. television, radio, newspapers, magazine etc. promotion channels. Because frequent advertisement promotion method can let any consumers often remember the product's brand, discounted price, style, color and image from advertisement content.

So, advertisement can be one part of consumer behavioral life-cycle. For example, when the television audiences often watch TV. Hence, when the brand of product advertisement often makes fun image and discounted message to let TV audiences to remember this brand of product, when they are watching TV. Then, it has possible to persuade any potential consumers to choose to buy this brand of any products or consume this brand of any services, due to its advertisement of discounted sale message is very attractive to every one to let this advertisement audience's attention to remember this brand of products or services are selling or serving in market at this moment. So, it is advertisement image behavior influences audiences to buy the brand's any products attractively and persuasively.

3. Raising electricity consumption from electricity user individual habit

For electricity use market case example, how to analyze people's behavior in consuming electricity using a behavioral economic framework ? Electricity consumption is modeled by the means of consumer's individual useful habit, electricity price, consumer satisfaction level, willingness to invest in new technologies, social interactions, and marketing strategies by the power utility. Because electricity is necessary to every home or electric vehicle users needs or businessmen office etc. different needs every day.

Power companies supply electricity to a region's homes and industries. However, electricity needs modernization of power system companies expect to increase price. Due to competitive factor, such as other fuel resource choices, outdated kind of energy electricity supply, and renewable fuel energy source competition.

Hence, applying behavioral economic concept, I assume electricity consumers will compare to electricity and other kinds of energy choices to weigh up the costs and benefits of all alternatives, aiming to maximize their benefits, before making a decision to choose to use electricity for their house electricity demand or electric vehicle or shop or factory manufacturing etc. function of different aspects of electricity users.

For example, electricity business clients, they aim to reduce cost, such as energy expenditure, when they use any energy to manufacture their products in factories. If they feel electricity is expensive price to compare other kinds of energy power supply. When, they feel that they can not earn much beneficial advantages to use electricity to produce their products. Otherwise, if they feel other any kinds of energy supply can replace electricity to give more benefits to compare electricity energy. Then, many business electricity users will change to use other kinds of energies to consume to replace electricity power.

However, electricity can have competitive ability in electric vehicles market, if many drivers feel environment protection is more important to compare vehicles will be popular to be driven, due to many drivers don't want air pollution. They will like gas vehicles. Hence, the main attribute from the consumer side is one their habit electricity consumption behaviors, satisfaction level, energy efficient interaction with the power utility.

Consequently how to predict electricity consumer's demand. The important factor is how to let electricity users to feel power companies are changing a reasonable level to compare other similar energy supply products. When electricity users feel electricity which can bring more benefits to compare other kinds of energy products. Then, in energy supply market, if the demanding number of electricity consumers can increase more than other kinds of energy demanding number. Then, it is right time to raise electricity price to charge electricity consumers. Hence, how to persuade electricity consumers to feel that they can have more benefits to compare other kinds of energy products. It is the main successful factor to electricity power supply companies.

● Consumer confidence is as a predictor of consumption spending

Behavioral economists believe it has link between confidence and economic decisions to cause consumers to choose spending, if the consumer has confidence to believe the product is worth to use, then who will accept to buy the product to use.

Concentrated on the conceptualization of confidence and its role in mode in theories of consumption. It also concerns on whether the confidence indicators contain any information beyond economic fundamentals. The concern is whether confidence can be explained by current and past value of variables, such as income, unemployment, inflation or consumption or in other way.

Whether confidence measures have any statistical significance in predicting economic outcomes once information from the above variables is used. Economic variable factor will also influence consumer confidence to decide consumption spending, e.g. real consumption expenditures (income, wealth or interest rate).

Finally, it will identify under which circumstances confidence indicates can be a good predictor of household consumption. Hence, survey is one good measurement method to predict whether how much every household has confidence to spend to consume the brand of products to use. Why is survey a good confidence consumption measurement prediction to every household in every country?

The reasons include survey can gather every household consumption habit history data to evaluate whether every survey person has how much confidence to consume the brand of products. Which in most cases correspond to periods where there are large changes in household survey indicators, liking during financial crises or geopolitical tensions to measure or predict whether the country's future good or bad economic condition factor will influence every household consumption desire in the year.

This modelling approach assumes that there is a certain (unknown) in confidence index changes beyond which confidence starts impacting consumption behaviors. So, sample household surveys can show the contribution of confidence in explaining consumption expenditures increases when household survey indicators feature large changes. So that confidence indicators can have some increasing predictive power during the survey investigation period in the year.

Other view point, surveys have been concerned on whether the confidence indicators contain any information beyond economic fundaments. The concern is whether confidence can be explained by current and past values of variables, such as income, unemployment, inflation or consumption or the other way. Whether confidence measures have any statistical significance in predicting economic outcomes once information from different external variable factors to influence the survey household group.

What is confidence in consumption survey ?

Confidence in consumption. For example, to measure whether how much degree of strong inflation in the economy, such as recessions and recoveries will influence the country's household confident consumption in the year. The surveys consumers' questions usually concern on major expenditures and changes in the respondent's financial situation, focus on job availability and current business conditions etc. questions. It is then possible that about consumer confidence depending on the relative performance of the variables that may be more relevant balances, with respect to the factors that determine unemployment and other labor market related issues. It aims to investigate whether those any one of variable factors will influence consumers general loss confident consumption desire in this year.

What is a confidence indicator ?

A confidence indicator is considered as an explanatory variable for consumption together with standard variables used on predicting consumption expenditure. However, the natural real personal consumption expenditure is unexpected and unpredicted easily.

In conclusion, consumption expenditure depends the consumer individual confidence. If the consumer has much confidence to feel this year economic change will be better and he/she is easily to find job, then he/she will accept consumption easily in this year. It seems financial wealth and unemployment etc. economic factors will influence every household consumption desire. So, survey is one kind of good psychological consumption prediction method to predict consumption spending for any country in the year. I recommend manufacturers may choose to apply survey method to attempt to enquire sample survey people to gather data to predict whether what degree of consumption desire to them and find solution methods to solve low degree of consumption desire challenge.

How to apply behavioral economy methods to influence employee individual psychology to achieve raise productivity of long term incentive intention?

Increasing salary is short term incentive productivity method. Behavioral economy assumes labors will choose to do beneficial behaviors to themselves when they feel their work behaviors can earn more benefits to themselves more than their employers in the organizations. Otherwise, if they feel their work behaviors can earn more benefits to their employers more than themselves. Then, they won't choose to do their work behaviors, e.g. raising productivities or work hard. Due to they feel work hard or raise productivities behaviors that only give more benefits to their employers more themselves.

Whether does cheap product price incentive consumption desire to influence effective consumption behavior? Whether is monetary increasing salary payment incentive labors might be willing to work on task? I feel raising labors productivities is similar to raise incentive consumption, which both have similar point, such as increasing salary payment or cheap product price is the main factor to influence incentive consumption or raising productivities. Hence, it seems monetary factor is not the main effort to encourage labors to work hard.

In labor's behavioral economic view point, for example, if an employer pays an employee more doing a task, who might be less willing to work on it, who might be less productive given whose efforts and who may enjoy the task less. If you want your employees to save more for retirement. You may want to give them fewer investment options. If you want them to engage more in a task, you might want offer them an additional alternative, instead of increasing salary to that task. Thus, increasing salary is not only method to encourage productivities of incentives.

How to improve the design of incentive structures to encourage productivities in any organizations?

Any monetary incentive can only encourage productivities in short term. It can not only encourage productivities in long term in any organizations. It is similar to cheap or discount product price can only attractive consumers to buy the product in short term, it can not attract consumers to choose to buy the product in long term, it prefers to have more options to encourage labors to incentive productivities, e.g. investing good beneficial retirement plans. Suggesting that employees do not have free disposal of their investment options. These standard incentives seem irrelevant raising salary monetary factor, they can be quite effective in inducing labors to take particular actions to incentive productivities in long term. Due to when they can hard work, then they have more beneficial retirement plans or investing plans for their retirement. It means when they can achieve the most effective or efficient productivities to the employer for long term. It will give better retirement benefits and investment benefits to the better or even the best performance of employees. Otherwise, the worst performance employees won't earn good retirement benefits and investment benefits, when their employers feel their perform very poor in the organizations in long term.

Hence, increasing salary level method is not one successful long term incentive method to persuade every employee to raise productivities or encourage excellent performance optional method. Increasing salary level is only similar to reduce product price and it is only short term encouragement to consumption or productivities method.

In conclusion, extrinsic monetary factor can not incentive labor's raising productivities more than every employee themselves intrinsic motivation to raise productivities as excellent performance in any organizations. Thus, organizations need to let employees to feel that they can give long term economic benefits to encourage their intrinsic motivation effort to be raised their productivities or performance more effective or efficient in order to achieve long term both win-win economic benefits to employees and employers both.

Building employees and managers kindly co-operational relationship method

If you are an economist, your employer has no without any financial incentive to encourage your economic research tasks in your organization. It is equally difficult to certify that such activity will contribute to your growth of human capital and increased productivity in research or teaching. The standard model, which explains employee's effort only through the way (determined by productivity), is therefore incomplete. In particular, it doesn't consider that incentives to work do not have to be monetary in other words, that there are other things besides the disutility of labor (Kamenica, 2012) and section 1.3 have.

Why will short term wage increasing method only influence short term labor supply to raise productivities? The effect of reference raising wage can be most easily identified on short term labor supply to raise productivities. For US, New York city taxi drivers case, they have to decide every day for low long they are going to offer their services, given the day-to-day variable ability of demand they face (peaking during bad weather and/or when big conferences and public events are taking place in the city).

In the standard model, houses worked should grow with any growth in demand for New York taxi drivers' services. (one day's earning will have only a negligible income effect in the longer run). And yet actual cabbies work less on a demand heavy day. One of possible explanations suggests that New York city taxi drivers expect a certain income, they have set themselves a specific target income, who expect to achieve every day. During low demand for their taxi services, then they work longer hours to reach the target, when during peak demand, their referential income is achieved quickly and they only work short hours. Elasticity of hours worked with respect to their earnings is therefore negative (Lamerer, Babcock,

Loewenstein, & Thaler, 1997).

However, taxi driver is either one self employment business or one taxi company employment driving service occupation. It is similar to other kinds of service jobs in societies. Servicing employees, such as waiters, salespeople, securities, customer services, bus drivers etc. different kinds of service occupations. They are not similar to manufacturing occupation to be applied how many amount of piece of products production to evaluate their productivities efforts. Thus these any one of service job nature is depended on their service performance to clients to feel their service performances are excellent to compare general service performance effort of service employees.

Considerably, respectively, I assume that if these service employees' managers can build kindly working environment, e.g. manager individual attitude and behavior can let their employees to feel happy to work together in their teams. Then, the managers' kindly as enthusiastic behaviors or attitudes will let every employee more positive encouragement of service attitude to serve their clients in their teams. Then, the client complaining number will be possible reduced, even none of any complains. Hence, building kindly relationship between managers and employees will raise excellent service performance to any organization service nature employees.

Can bonus method encourage service performance to be raised ?

In service job nature of bonus method can also raise employees' overall productivities or service performance. For example, when employees got a provisional bonus before the start of the workweek, but were warned that they would lose it on payday, unless they achieve the productivities or excellent service performance norm, they worked more productivities or let many clients to satisfy their service performance. Hence, managers can achieve bonus plan to compensate any excellent productivity or excellent services to them. Then, they can let clients to feel their service performance more satisfactory than employees of a control group who were merely given the standard promise to receive a bonus upon achieving the norm.

The effort was relatively small, however, productivity grew 1%. Interestingly, the effect of a loss was stronger when how teams were rewarded this way, social pressure came to bear on the less productivity team members. When the team members won't earn any bonus. So, long-term productivity gains were achieved through bonuses paid by excellent performance compensation method to compare to low service performance employees receiving no bonuses at all.

Economic views of human motivation nature

There are only two main types of economic actors and by making simplifying assumptions about how these types of actors behave and interact. The two basic sets of actors in this model are firms, which are assumed in this model are firms, which are assumed to maximize their profits from producing and selling products and services, households, which are assumed to maximize their utility (or satisfaction) from consuming products and services.

It seems any employees will choose to do behaviors to achieve to earn much benefits from their organizations. The models of economic behaviors that consider considerate employees' choice of goals, the actions they take to achieve these goals and the limitations and influences that affect their choices and actions.

For university students choose which universities to study case, suppose that any college enrollment students are deciding which courses to study. Thus, it implies that if the university can provide many different kinds of suitable or right courses to any college enrollment students to choose to study. It means that if the university can provide many different kinds of courses to enrollment students to choose to study. Then, it will have much chance to attract enrollment students to choose this university to study. It's competition can be raised by many courses choice factor. but, in fact, it is not absolute right, although the university can provide many courses to provide to enrollment students to choose to study. But, it is not guarantee to represent it must attract many students to enroll this university to study.

For example, suppose that college enrollment students are deciding which courses to choose to study. Although, it has right course to prepare to these enrollment students to choose to study. But, they see a summary of evaluations from hundreds of other students indicating that a certain course is very good in this university. Then, suppose that they match a video interview of just one student to give a negative review of this university of the course. Even when students were told in advance that such a negative review was worse to this university of the course. They tended to be more influenced by the negative review than the summary of hundreds of evaluations, even although such behavior seems irrational. Hence, although many right courses choice has much chance to attract students to enroll this university to study. But, if its bad educational quality from this course from negative review factor, which will influence the enrollment students number to be reduced.

It implies that students will compare this university's the course educational quality whether is better or worse to compare other universities' similar course educational quality, even this university's this course fee whether is reasonable in educational market. This is cost and beneficial comparison behavioral economy principle to all enrollment students before they decide to choose which universities.

Hence, this case implies that universities how to train teachers' teaching skills to let students to feel that they can learn new knowledge from their teaching staffs absolutely. It means how to raise education training skills to raise teachers' teaching performance. It is very important factor to influence the university's teaching development success. So, many courses choice is not important factor to attract many students to enroll the university. Otherwise, although the university can not provide many courses to let students to enroll, but it's teachers can provide excellent teaching service to teach whose students. This is important factor to attract many students to choose to enroll this university to study.

Under-level productive efficiency and low-consumption desire behavioral economic influences

In behavioral economic influence view point, I feel that under-level productive efficiency is the represent low production number to the manufacturer as well as low-consumption desire is not represent less consumers demands or customers lose confidence to the product.

On the one hand, I shall apply behavioral economic method to analyze why under productive efficiency is not represent low production number influence. Otherwise, I feel under-productive efficiency will have possible to increase production number after the manufacturer can review what factor(s) to influence under-productive efficiency.

I shall give reasons to explain as below:

As Jim, P. & Brendan. M. (2013) indicated who had ever been experiencing failure to do their businesses. Although, they had lost a million dollars, but they felt that they can be taught to learn undiscovered knowledge to know how to do their businesses successful by their wrong judgement and decision learning experience. They explained that " in ll risk taking, speculation, business ventures, entrepreneurial activities, it is the loss side on which you must focus first. This is even true for gambling, the gambler determines how much he's willing to bet, and loss, before the game is played. He doesn't wait for the game to end and then let the croupier or dealer assign his wager for him. How do you determine the downside, and how do you control or minimize it? With objective decision making and a plan that has as its starting point the stop-loss parameters"

Hence, it explains any business will have under-level productive efficiencies and low consumption desire business risk. However, to any one entrepreneur, who needs to know it is one game between the himself/herself and whose clients. They also need to know with objective decision making and a plan that has as its starting point.

Hence, I assume that if the entrepreneur has wrong decision to cause under-level productive efficiency, it is possible that, due to there is no enough employee number to manufacture the product or many employees are not skillful to manufacture all product in normal time or many employees are lazy etc. different factors to cause under-level productivities. However, when they discover their productivities are very low to compare similar competitors their employees' productivities and efficiencies. Then, they can attempt to find what factor(s) to cause low productivities and low efficiencies. it is possible that any one among of these factors case. They include many employees' lazy to influence low productivities or there is no enough employee number or many employees are not skillful to manufacture their products in production process.

Hence, wrong decision or plan is not represent failure. Otherwise, it can give chance to let the entrepreneur to learn whether what the factor(s) is (are) to cause low productivities and low efficiencies in whose product manufacturing process. As I feel that under-level productive efficiency is not represent low production number. Because I assume that if one worker lacks enough skills and manufacturing experiences to manufacture the product, but who can spend less time to manufacture the product and whose spending manufacturing time is same to the another owning enough skillful worker's time to do the product. Hence, I believe that the product quality from the low-skillful worker's manufacturing skill, it's quality will be worse to compare to the product quality from the high skillful worker's manufacturing skill. Hence, if the low skillful worker needs to spend much time to produce the product, but the product quality can be same to the high skillful worker's product quality. It means that it is sure because the low skillful worker has no excellent skill to compare to the high skillful worker to produce the product. Hence, his manufacturing spending time must be longer than the high skillful worker's time. It implies that the low skillful worker spends less time to raises high production number, but his product must be poor quality to sell. Then, his fast and efficient manufacturing speed that is not achieve economic beneficial to the organization's manufacturing process, e.g. less electricity spends to manufacture the product. Otherwise, the low skillful worker's fast and efficient manufacturing speed of behavior will raise the organization's cost in manufacturing process because consumers would not like to choose to buy any low quality product when they can choose which similar products to compare which one has the best quality and cheap price to buy.

Hence, efficient production is not the main factor to influence the business's success. Otherwise, good quality of the product factor is more important to compare it to influence the business's success.

On the other hand, I shall apply behavioral economic theory to analyze why low-consumption desire is not represent consumer demand lose to the business. As Jim. P. & Brendan. M. (2013) also identified " rather than looking for success to follow, who explained the formula for failure to avoid. As an Wang, founder of Wang laboratories said " it is my belief that there are no secret to success." The formula for failure is not lack of knowledge, brains, skills or hard work and it's not lack of luck, it's personalizing losses, especially of preceded by a string of wins or profits. It's refusing to acknowledge and accept the reality of a loss when it starts to occur because to so so would reflect negatively on you."

Thus, as whose feeling to explain why low-consumption desire is not represent less consumers demands or customers lose confidence to the product. The reasons include the causes of low-consumption desire are possible due to worse economic environment factor influences consumption desire to be reduced. It is not due to whether the product price is too high or quality is worse to compare others. Hence, as Jim & Brendan indicated the formula for business failure is not lack of knowledge, brains, skills or hard work and it's not lack of luck. It's not lack of luck. It's personalizing losses, means its reflecting to knowledge and accept the reality of a loss when it starts to occur. As it is applied to explain why low-consumption desire is not represent less consumers demands or customers lose confidence to the product. It's possible that external economic environment changing worse factor to cause the business personalizing losses, it is not reflect who lacks knowledge, skill, hard work factors to cause failure. Hence, ho to predict when and how and why economic environment changes worse will be important factor to predict when and how and why consumption behavioral changes to cause business's success.

● Demand and supply theory solves organizational problems

Any organizations can let salespeople feel happy to sell their products. Then their sale performance will also raise. The question concerns that how to make them to feel happy to help the organization to sell their products? I shall explain some methods as below:

How to manage sales for predictable revenue? In order to hold salespeople sale psychology whether they feel happy or unhappy, executives need to understand the essential activities, sales managers must focus on to be analysts for change, foster continuous improvement and create a sales culture that drives results. Sale executives need to know how to achieve top objectives of sales management is to drive sales, capture new revenue and exceed monthly sales and margin objectives, e.g. performing sale straregy development with each salesperson on Monday morning at a minimum, and in a formal one-on-one meeting during the week;using strategy tools and questioning techniques to ensure the prospects are qualified and the strategy is valid; knowing the ratio between future values and future monthly quotos to raise sale opportunities; six month on-going sale plan aims to make sure there are coordinated to achieve sale to various market segments; developing on ongoing series of networking events to build market awareness in order to ensure all salespeople attend specific events involved in networking by salespeople to, understanding the market how to influence salespeople sale method to sale number, understanding trends and seeking some channels to raise additional sales opportunities; how to create trained or warm sale environment to let sales teams feel happy to sell.

How to design and utilize efficient control sale procedures? The sale cycle procedure may include these market activities, such as advertising, sales promotion, market research, physical distribution, pricing , sale place, sale staffs seeking. SO, any organizations need have good sale planning, direction and control of the personnel, selling activities of a business with including recruiting, selecting, training, rating, supervising, paying or reward system, motivating strategy , as all these tasks apply to the personnel sales-force.

The factors may influence salespeople psychology, they may include fair income reward system, or appreciation methods and sale career development plan to every salesperson. It aims to encourage them to achieve the highest sale effort. Anymore, methods to train sale managers have the right direction to guide, lead and motivate their salespeople, e.g. knowledge of salespeople psychology needs how to satisfy them, understanding why they choose to do or act themselves sale behaviors in order to improve their weakness to motivate salespeople to achieve company's sale target goal every month easily, e.g. raising profitability, sales volume, market share, growth and corporate image building raise clients' confidence to choose to buy this company's any products more easily.

The sales organization is required for the following purposes, they may include: enabling top-management, to devote to more time in policy making for the growth and expansion of business to divide and fix authority among the subordinates , so that they may shirk work, to avoid repetition of duties and functions, so that there may not be any confusion among them to locate responsibility of each and every employee , so that they can complete the whole work in stipulated time, if not then the particular person must be responsible, to establish the sales effort to enforce proper supervision of sales force.

What does the concept of salespeople replacement value mean? What is a sales force turnover management tool? Sales force turnover is defined as the rate at which salespeople leave an organizations, resignations, retirements or dismissals. So, if the organization can raise the sales force turnover ratio, because many salespeople can be promoted or the retirement, or the sales force turnover ratio raising reasons as well as they are not resignation or dismissal reasons. I believe that the organization ought have good sale environment and reasonable reward and welfare strategy to let its salespeople feel happy to help this company to sell its products every day.

However, sales management's actions have direct or indirect effects to impact on turnover. Direct effects may include the firm's firing or dismiss policy. The indirect effects on sale turnover may include new salesperon recruiting and selecting policies affect the quality and performance of the sale force as well as the speed at which salespeople are replaced. The same policies have an impact on the sales force turnover rate through the characteristics of the newly recurited salespersons and the promotion , training, retraining policies, support, supervision, compensation. ALl of those factors have an impact on salesperson's personal satisfaction or dissatisfaction absolutely. So, any sale organizations need to concern how and why whether any one of above these factors may influence their salespeople how to perform or act sale behaviors in order to excite their sale number more effective in long term.

How to achieve sale force management effectively? Sale management is one strategy to many organizations, because organizations expect their salespeople can only raise product sale number. So , they will consider whetther how to implement the sale management strategy to be the most suitable to themselves sale organizations in order to excite their sale teams to sell their products to achieve sale growth aim effectively. So for organization's long term sale growth development, it seems that one excellent sale management strategy can help the organization has stable sale number growth in long term possible.

However, the term " selling" includes a variety of sales situations and activities. For example, those sales positions where the sales representative is required primarily to deliver the product to the customer on a regular or periodic basis. The emphasis is this type of sales activity is very different to the sales position where the sales representative is dealing with sales of capital equipment to industrial purchasers. IN additions some sales representatives deal only in export markets whereas others sell direct to customers in their homes. So, sale organizations need to sell to local or overseas market as well as its target customer is businessmen or individual consumer or both in order to implement to choose their most suitable sale management strategy to train their salespeople more effective or achieving sale growth objective only. Because these its sale major target and where sale market place both factors will influence how it ought train its salespeople, so any organization's training method ought be influenced to change by whom is its major sale target and where is its major sale market location factors.

How to know the psychology of salesmanship? WHen the organization can predict or find reasons to explain why its salespeople feel unhappy to help
this organization to sell its products. Then, it can attempt to improve its weaknesses in order to let its salespeople to feel more sale service satisfactory feeling to continue to help this organization to sell its products. THen, it won't need not often to train or recruit new salespeople to replace its old salespeople in consequence. How to know what its salespeoples' real need in order to raise their sale service satisfactory feeling ?

Psychology means that " science of the mind" and psychology plays to important part in business and it is quite worth to bring to influence any organization salespeoples' posivitive or negative sale emotion in their every sale process between themselves and their every client in personal. For example, if the salesperson often have negative emotion or he feels unhappy in every sale process, then he will encounter or increase many times of sale failure possibilities. He will feel that he is one poor verbal advertiser or seller or promotor to help his organization to promote its products to sell again as well as he will lose confidence to sell any products next sale chance, because his failure sale experiences are accumulated to influence his sale emotion to be poor or difficult sale.

Hence, the poor performance salesperson needs have more successful sale experiences to compensate his / her prior many sale failure times feeling, if the organization hopes this poor performance salesperson can raise sale number easily. Overall, any organizations need to concern how to improve or raise the more failure times of sale experience salespeoples' sale techniques or methods or attitudes more than choose to fire or dismiss them as well as finding another new salesperson to replace him/her. Because it is possible that the salesperson 's poor sale performance that is not due to himself/herself poor sale effort and sale knowledge or lacking sale experience to the product, it may be due to the poor sale team cooperation relationship , feeling poor or not comfortable sale physcial shop environment, poor sale manager and other salespeople working relationship, the sale manager lacks leadership effort, poor family relationship etc. external factors more than himself/herself personal poor or negative emotion or poor health etc. personal factors. Hence, the organization ought enquire him/her why he/she feels unhappy to sell its products and it needs to attempt to find methods to solve his/her challenges immediately. If his/her challenges can be solved. It is possible that his/her sale efforts can be also raised for. So, if the organization can know how to utilize positive sale emotion psychological methods to predict or know why and how every salesperson perform his/her sale behavior in whose daily sale tasks, then it can concentrate on implementing effective and the most suitable sale training to raise their sale abilities more easily.

However, the sale training may include: How to build or improve long term good salesperson and his/her customer sale service relationship between every salesperson and every client in every buying and selling cycle process, how to using right communicating styleds for better understanding every client's real needs, powers and negotiating, e.g. every salesperson needs to review why there are many clients do not choose to buy any products from his sale presentation or promotion, finding every time sale failure reasons can let the salesperson makes himself/herself sale failure reasons evaluation or judgement in order to find what is the major reason influences his/her sale failure, e.g. lacking product knowledge, he/she often let many clients to feel that he lacks patience to listen the client's enquiry or feedback, his sale presentation is not attractive to let many clients like to stay longer time to listen his sale presentation in whole sale process, the salesperson himself/herself emotion is negative and he /she can let many clients feel he / she is not happy or does not enjoy to sell this product from himself/herself face impression or sale behavior impression easily, lacking enough sale techniques to persuade his/her clients why he/she ought choose to buy this product in whole sale process etc. these factors may influence the salesperson's sale failure chance to be raised. Hence sales manager ought need to spend long time to meet the poor sale performance salesperson to discuess what his/her sale challenges are the most major to influence his/her every sale successful chance in order to improve his/ her sale performance more successfully.

IN conclusion, the reasons why salespeople often encounter sale failure possibilities. The factors may include these aspects, such as they lask the desire to help customers to make satisfactory purchase decisons, they only concern how to achieve sale final objective or aim only, it will cause clients feel they do not real concern their real needs. They only concern to sell the product in success. They do not know how to describe the product whether what characteristics or features it owns accurately in order to increase sale chance to persudade them to make final decision to by the product, they do not attempt to participate the whole sale process to help them to choose the most right product in order to satisfy their any purcahse needs, they ought avoid deceptive or manipulative influence tactics, avoid the use of high pressure sales techniques etc. Thus, if any organizations can spend time to investigate what factors cause why any one of salespeople choose perform his/her sale behavior often in order to know or understand their salespeople' sale psychology absolutely. Then, I believe that their sale number will only grown more easily.

TWO

TRAVEL ENTERTAINMENT MARKET

What factors can influence travel behavioural consumption

Prediction travel behavioral consumption from psychology view and computer statistic view.

How to predict travel consumption? It is one question to any travel agents concern to use what methods which can predict how many numbers of travelers where who will choose to go to travel more accurately. I think that who can consider how to predict travel behavioral consumption from psychology view and computer science view both.

On the psychology view, It has evidence to support the relationship between self-identify threat and resistance to change travel behavior to any travelers, controlling for whose past travelling behavior, resistance to change if a psychological phenomenon of long standing interest in many applied branches of psychology. Past travelling behavior has been acknowledged as a predictor of future action. Such as travelling behavior that is experienced as successful is likely to be repeated and may lead to habitual patterns. Some psychologists differentiate habit between two concepts, such as goal oriented and automatic oriented both. Although repeated past travelling behavior is addition goal oriented and automatic oriented. Further non-deliberative nature of habit may make appeals to judge and to predict future individual traveler's behaviour accrately.

However, repeated travelling behavior without a necessary constraint of goal orientation and automatic oriented both. So, it seems that psychological factor can influence any individual traveler why and how who choose to decide whose travelling behaviour.

On the computer statistic view, structural equation modeling is an extremely flexible linear-in-parameters multivariate statistical modeling technique. It has been used in modeling travel behavior and values since about 1980 year. It is a software method to handle a large number of variables, as well as unobserved variables specified as linear combinations (weighted averages) of the observed variable.

●

Whether climate change can influence travelling behaviours.

The flexibility of human travelling behavior is at least the result of one such mechanism, our ability to travel mentally in time and entertain potential future. Understanding of the impacts is holidays, particularly those involving travel. Using focus groups research to explores tourists' awareness of the impacts of travel own climate change, examines the extent to which climate change features in holiday travel decisions and identifies some of the barriers to the adoption of less carbon intensive tourism practices. The findings suggest many tourists don't consider climate change when planning their holidays. The failure of tourists to engage with the climate change to impact of holidays, combined with significant barriers to behavioral change, presents a considerable challenge in the tourism industry.

Tourism is a highly energy intensive industry and has only recently attracted attention as an important contributions to climate change through greenhouse gas emissions. It has been estimated that tourism contributes 5% of global carbon dioxide emissions. There have been a number of potential changes proposed for reducing the impact of air travel on climate change. These include technological changes, market based changes and behavioral changes. However, the role that climate change plays in the holiday and travel decisions of global tourists. How the global tourists of the impacts travel has on climate change to establish the extent to which climate change, considerations features in holiday travel decision making processes and to investigate the major barriers to global tourists adopting less carbon intensive travel practices. Whether tourists will aware the impacts that their holidays and travel have on climate changes.

When, it comes to understand indvidual traveler's behavioral change, wide range of conceptual theories have been developed, utilizing various social, psychological, subjective and objective variables in order to model travel consumption behavior. These theories of travel behavioral change operate at a number of different levels, including the individual level, the interpersonal level and community level. Whether pro-environmental behavior can be used to predict travel consumption behavior in a climate change. However, the question of what determines pro-environmental behavior in such a complex one that it can not be visualized through one single framework or diagram.

Despite the potentially high risk scenario for the tourism industry and the global environment, the tourism and climate change ought have close relationship. Whether what are the important factors and variables which can limit tourism? e.g. money, time, family problem, extreme hot or cold weather change, air ticket price, journey attraction etc. variable factors. Mention of holidays and travel were deliberately avoided in the recruitment process, so as not to create a connection factor to influence traveler's individual mind. However, the dismissal of alternative transportation modes can be conceived as either a structural barrier, in the sense that flying is perhaps the only realistic option to reach long-haul holiday destination, or a perceived behavioral control barriers in that an individual perceives flying as the only option open to whom. The transportation tool factor will be depend to extent on the distance to the destination. This can also be interpreted in a social perspective as an intention with the resources available where much international tourism is structured around flying. To increase the availability of different transportation modes, tourists could choose holiday destination closer to home.

Finally, also how to predict future travel behavioural consumption. I feel that travel agents need to predict whether any country's random daily variation of weather factor is also important to influence travel behaviour. e.g. in weather, temperature, rainfall adn snowfall with traffic accidents factors will have relationship to cause travel demand. Some scientists estimate suggest that when warmed temperatures and reduced snowfall are associated with a moderate decline in non-fatal accidents, they are also associated with a significant increase in fatal accidents. Thus increase in fatalities and temperature. Half of the estimated effect of temperature on fatalities is due to changes in the exposure to pedestrians, bicyclists and motorcyclists as temperature increase. So, if any countries have rainfall, snowfall and low temperature to cause traffic accidents, whether this accident occurrence will influence the travelers who liking climb snow hills, riding bicycle, running sports who will avoid to travel to these countries' bad weather after occurs. So, why I feel that this natural climate factor will also be one serious factor to influence travel behavioral consumption.

● Whether individual habitual behaviour can influence travelling behaviour : e.g. renting
travel transportation tools

Whether habit can be intended to predict of future travel behavior to people are creatures of habits. Many of human's everyday goal-directed behaviors are performed in a habitual fashion, the transportation made and route one takes to work, one's choice of breakfast. Habits are formed when using the some behavior frequently and a similar consistency in a similar context for the some purpose whether the individual past travel consumption model will be caused a habit to whom. e.g. choosing whom travel agent to buy air ticket or traveling package; choosing the same or similar countries' destinations to go to travel ; choosing the business class or normal (general) class of quality airlines to catch planes. Does habitual rent traveling car tools use not lead to more resistance to change of travel mode? It has been argued that past behavior is the best predictor of future behavior to travel consumption. If individual traveler's past consumption behavior was always reasoned, then frequency of prior travel consumption behavior should only have an indirect link to the individual traveler's behavior. It seems that renting travel car tools to use is a habit example. So, a strong rent traveling car tools useful habit makes traveling mode choice. People with a strong renting of traveling car tools of habit should have low motivation to attend to gather any information about public transportation in their choice of travelling country for individual or family or friends members during their traveling journeys.

Even when persuasive communication changes the traveler whose attitudes and intention, in the case of individual traveler or family travelers with a strong renting travel car tools habit. It is difficult to change whose travel behaviors to choose to catch public transportation in whose any trips in any countries. However, understanding of travel behavior and the reasons for choosing one mode of transportation over another. The arguments for rent traveling car tools to use, including convenience, speed, comfort and individual freedom and well known. Increasingly, psychological factors include such as, perceptions, identity, social norms and habit are being used to understand travel mode choice. Whether how many travel consumers will choose to rent traveling car tools during their trips in any countries. It is difficult to estimate the numbers. As the average level of renting travel car tools of dependence or attitudes to certain travel package policies from travel agents. Instead different people must be treated in different ways because who are motivated in different ways and who are motivated by different travel package policies ways from travel agents.

In conclusion, the factors influence whose traveler's individual behavior either who chooses to rent traveling car tools or who chooses to catch public transportation when who individual goes to travel in alone trip or family trip. It include influence mode choice factors, such as social psychology factor and marketing on segmentation factor both to influence whose transportation choice of behavior in whose trip.

● How to determine future travel behavior from past travel experience and perceptions of risk and safety for the benefits to travel consumers?

How to determine future travel behavior from past travel experience and perceptions of risk and safety for the benefits to travel consumers? Why does individual traveler avoid certain destination(s) is(are) as relevant to tourist decision making as why who chooses to travel to others. Perceptions of risk and safety and travel experience are likely to influence travel decisions. If travel agents had efforts to predict future travel behavior to guess whether travelers will feel where is(are) risk and unsafe to cause who does not choose to go to the country to travel. Then, the travel agents will avoid to choose to spend much time to design the different traveling package to attract their potential travel consumers to choose to travel. The reason is because in the case of individual traveler's tourism experience, the traveler whose past disappointment travel experience (psychological risk) will be a serious threat to the traveler's health or life (health, physical or terrorism risk). The past safety or unhealthy risk to the country(countries) will influence the traveler decides to choose not to go to the countries(country) to travel again in the future.

●

What is push and pull factors to influence any
traveler who chooses where is whose preferable travelling destination.

How to predict individual traveler's behavioral intention of choosing a travel destination. Understanding why people travel and what factors influence their behavioral intention of choosing a travel destination is beneficial to tourism planning and marketing. In general, an individual's choice of a travel destination into two forces. The first force is the push factor that pushes an individual away from home and attempt to develop a general desire to go somewhere, without specifying where that may be. The other force is the pull factor that pull an individual toward in destination, due to a region-specific or perceived attractiveness of a destination. The respective push and pull factors illustrate that people travel because who are pushed by whose internal motives and pulled by external forced of a destination. However, the decision making process leading to the choice of a travel destination is a very complex process. For example, a Taiwanese traveler who might either choose new travel destination of Hong Kong or another old travel Asia destinations again or who also might choose any one of Western country, as a new travel destination. The travel agents can predict where who will have intention to choose to travel from whose past behavior and attitude, subjective and perceived behavioral control model.

The factors influence where is the traveler choice, include personal safety, scenic beauty, cultural interest, climate changing, transportation tools, friendliness of local people, price of trip, trip package service in hotels and restaurants, quality and variety of food and shopping facilities and services etc. needs. So, whose factors will influence where is the individual travel's choice. It seems every traveler whose choice of travel process, will include past behavior. e.g. travelling experience, travelling habit, then to choose the best seasoned travelling action to satisfy whose travel needs. This process is the individual traveler's psychological choice process, who must need time to gather information to compare concerning of different travel packages, destination scene, climate change, transportation tools available to the destination, air ticket price etc. these factors, then to judge where is the best right destination to travel in the right time.

●

Why expectation, motivation and attitude factor can influence travelling behaviour.

Social psychology is concerned with gaining insight into the psychological of socially relevant behaviors and the processes. For instance, on a global level bad influence to global warming, it influences some countries extreme cold or hot bad climate changing occurrence, then it ought influence some travelers' behavioral decision to change their mind to choose some countries to go to travel at the moment which do not occur extreme hot or cold climate (temperature). e.g. above than 40 degree in summer or below than 0 degree in winter. Due to the extreme climate changing environment in the countries, it will cause them to feel uncomfortable to play during their trips. So, the global warming causes to climate changing factor will influence the numbers of travel consumption to be reduced possibly. This is global climate changing environment factor influences to bad or uncomfortable social psychological feeling to global travelers' mind of traveling decision. What is individual traveler expectation, motivation and attitude? Tourism sector includes inbound (domestic) tourism and outbound (overseas) tourism both incomes to any countries. According to recent article, a tourist behavior model has been developed, called the expectation, motivation and attitude (EMA) model (Hsu et al., 2010).

This model focuses on the pre-visit stage of tourists by modeling the behavioral process by incorporating expectation, motivation and attitude. Travel motivation is considered as an essential component of the behavioral process, which has been increasing attention from the travel; industry. The economic approach defines "tourism" is an identifiable nationally important industry. It includes the component activities of transportation, accommodation, recreation, food and related service. So, tourism behavioral consumption is concerned the individual tourist's usual habituate of the industry which responds to whose needs, and of the impacts that both the tourist and the tourism industry have on the socio-cultural, economic and physical environment.

However, travel motivation means how to understand and predict factors that influence travel decision making. According to Backman and others (1995, p.15), motivation is conceptually viewed as " a state of need, a condition that services as a driving force to display different kind of behavior toward certain types of activities, developing preferences, arriving at some expected satisfactory outcome." So, motivation and expectancy which has close relationship to any tourist before who decided to do any tourism of behavior. Some economists confirmed motivation and expectancy which has relations, such as expectation of visiting an outbound destination has a direct effect on motivation to visit the destination; motivation has a direct effect on attitude toward visiting the destination; expectation of visiting the outbound destination has a direct affect on attitude toward visiting the destination and motivation has a mediating effect on the relationship in between expectation and attitude.

● How to use qualitative of travel behavioural method to predict future travel consumption.

I also suggest to use qualitative of travel behavioural method to predict future travel consumption. Methods such as focus groups interviews and participant observer techniques can be used with quantitative approaches on their own to fill the gaps left by quantitative techniques. These insights have contributed to the development of increasingly sophisticated models to forecast travel behavior and predict changes in behavior in response to change in the transportation system. First, survey methods restrict not only the question frame but the answer frame as well, anticipating the important issues and questions and the responses. However, these surveys methods are not well suited to exploratory areas of research where issues remain unidentified and the researched seek to answer the question "why?". Second, data collection methods using traditional travel diaries or telephone recruitment can under represent certain segments of the population, particularly the older persons with little education, minorities and the poor. Before the survey, focus group for example can be used to identify what socio-demographic variables to include in the survey, how best to structure the diary, even what incentives will be most effective in increasing the response rate. After the survey, focus, focus groups can be used to build explanations for the survey results to identify the "why" of the results as well as the implications. One Asia Pacific survey research result was made by tourism market investigation before. It indicated the travel in Asia Pacific market in the past, had often been undertaken in large groups through leisure package sold in bulk, or in large organized business groups, future travelers will be in smaller groups or alone, and for a much wider range of reasons. Significant new traveler segments, such as female business traveler. The small business traveler and the senior traveler, all of which have different aspirations and requirements from the travel experience.

Moreover, Asia tourism market will start to exist behaviors in the adoption of newer technologies, a giving the traveler new ways to manage the travel experience, creating new behaviors. This with provide new opportunities for travel providers. The use of mobile devices, smartphones, tablets etc. and social media are the obvious findings to become an integral part of the travel experience. Thus, quality method can attempt to predict Asia Pacific tourism market development in the future.

However, improving the predictive power of travel behavior models and to increase understanding travel behavior which lies in the use of panel data(repeated measures from the same individuals). Whereas, cross-sectional data only reveal inter-individual differences at one moment in time, panel data can reveal intra-individual changes over time. In effect, panel data are generally better suited to understand and predict (changes in) travel behavior. However, a substantial proportion was also observed to transition between very different activity/travel patterns over time, indicating that from one year to the next, many people renegotiated their activity/travel patterns.

● How to apply advanced traveler information systems (ATIS) to predict future travelling behaviour.

Nowadays, information can impact on traveler behavior and network performance. For example, when steadily growing levels of vehicle ownership and vehicle miles traveled information has been identified as a potential strategy towards man aging travel demand, optimizing transportation networks and better utilizing available capacity. Toward, this goal to predict further tourist behavioral consumption. Many countries, government tourism development institutes has applied advanced traveler information systems (ATIS) which travel behavior models and high-fidelity network performance models made increasingly feasible through the rapid advances in computer power. Crucial components of this problem domain are the modeling of individual tourist drivers' response to travel information and the development accurate guidance of relevance to real would trip makers. So, this advanced traveler information systems (ATIS) can assist the tourist who like to rent travelling car tools to travel in any countries own free traveler information systems service conveniently. Also, this travel information system can be intended to assist travelers to make better travel choices. e.g. this system can improve the decision making of individual traveler rather than improvements of network performance overall. So, we need to understand how tourists make their travel plans. Also, understanding decision process that lead to booking of the trip is equally important, as it allows of a potential behavior.

●

How does online tourism sale channel can influence traveling consumption of behaviour.

Nowadays, internet is popular, it seems that booking air ticket behavior of using internet is predicted to influence overall tourism air tickets payment method. Tourism industry has grown in the previous several decades. Despite its global impact, questions related to better understanding of tourists and whose habits. Using online travel air ticket booking benefits include booking electronic air tickets can be made from entering any electronic travel agents websites in the short time and electronic travel ticket payers do not need leave home, who can pay visa card to pre booking any electronic travel ticket from online channel conveniently.

How to analyze activity based travel demand ? Nowadays, human are concerning the traffic congestion and air quality deterioration, the supply oriented focus of transportation planning has expanded to include how to manage travel demand within the available transportation supply. Consequently, there has been an increasing interest in travel demand management strategies, such as congestion pricing that attempts to change aggregate travel demand. The prediction aggregate level, long term travel demand to understanding disaggregate level (i.e. individual levels) behavioral responses to short term demand policies, such as ride sharing incentives, congestion pricing and employer based demand management schemes, alternate work schedules, telecommuting limitation of travel agent traditionally work nature shall influence oriented trip based travel modelling passenger travel demand indirectly.

Finally, online travel purchase will be popular to influence the number of travel behavioural consumption nowadays. Any travel package products can be sold from websites to attract travellers to choose to prebook air ticket for any trips conveniently. In the past ten years, the internet has become the predominant carrier of all types of information and transactions. Regarding travel decisions, internet has also become an important sales channels for the travel industry, because it is associated with comparably lower distribution and sales costs, but also because ir adapts to hign supply and demand dynamics in this industry. Consequently, the travel and tourism industry tries to increase the internet sale specific share of sales volumes. So, internet sale channel has changed travel consumption behavioural pattern and characteristics and travel experience. For example, Switzerland has one of the highest population-to-computer ratio in Europe. It is also one of the most highly internet penetrated countries in terms of use of the WWW on a day-to-day basis, with more than 75 percent of the population older than 14 years using the WWW daily (ICT, 2005).

The reason of booking online tourism may include: convenience, fast transaction, finding traveling package choice easily, more airline seats available. So, online booking tourism will influence the traditional tourism agents visiting of sales and air tickets and travelling package numbers to be decreased. Finally, the online booking tourism market shares will be expanded to more than traditional tourism agents visits sale market in the future one day. So, the travel agents who still use the traditional tourism visiting sale channel which ought raise whose features to compare to differ to online tourism sale channel if these traditional touriam agents want to keep competitive ability in tourism industry for long term.

●

Actively based patterns of urban population of travel behavioural prediction method.

Actively based patterns of urban population. It is a method of motivational framework means in which societal constraints and inherent individual motivations interact to shape activity participation patterns. It can be used to predict one city or urban the numbers of travel demand in the year. It has two elements: First, capability constraints refer to constraints are imposed by biological needs, such as eating and sleeping and/or resources, such as income, availability of cars etc. to undertake the urban or city's family activities in the year. Second, coupling constraints define where, when and the duration of planning activities that are to be pursued with other individuals. So, this method needs to gather information (data) to get the relationship between activities, travel and spending work time and space time to evaluate whether there are how many families who have real needs to spend time to go to travel in the year.

●

What is trip based versus activity based approaches?

What is trip based versus activity based approaches? The fundamental difference between the trip-based and activity based approaches is that the former approach directly focuses on trips without explicit recognition of the motivation or reason for the trips and travel. The activity based approach , on the other hand, views travel as a demand derived from the need to pursue travel activities. So, it is better understand the individual or family behavior basis for individual or family travelling decision regarding participation in travelling activities in certain places or cities or countries at given times and hence the resulting travel needs. This behavioral basis includes all the factors that influence the why, how, when and where of performed activities and resulting individuals and household, the cultural/social norms of the community and the travel surrounding environment.

Another difference between the two approaches is in the way travel is represented. The trip based approach represents travel as a collection of trips. Each trip is considered as independent of other trips, without considering the inter-relationship in the choice attributes , such as time, destination and mode of different trips. As tours are chains of trips beginning and ending at a same location , say home or work. The tour based representation helps maintain the consistency across and capture the interdependency and consistency of the modeled choice attributed among the trips of the same tour.

In addition to the tour based representation of travel, the activity based approach focuses on sequences or patterns of activity participation and travel behavior, using the whole day or longer periods of time is the unit of analysis. Such as approach can address travel demand management issues through an examination of how people modify their activity participation, for example, will individuals substitute more out-of-home activities for in home activities in the evening of who arrived early form work due-to a work schedule change?

The major difference between trip based and the activity based approaches is in the way, the time dimension of activities and travel is considered. In the trip based approach, time is reduced to being simply a cost making a trip and a day's viewed as a combination, defined peak and off peak time periods. On the other hand, activity based approach views individuals' activity travel patterns are a result of their time use decisions with a continuous time domain. As individuals have 24 hours in a day or multiples of 24 hours for longer periods of time and decide how to use that travel among or allocate that time to activities and travel and with who, subject to their socio-demographic, transportation system and other and scheduling of trips. So, determining the impact of travel demand management policies on time use behavior is an important step to assessing the impact of such policies on individual travel behavior. The final major difference between this two approaches relates to the level of aggregation. In the trip based approach, most aspect of travel, e.g. number of trips etc. are analyzed at an aggregate level.

Consequently, trip based methods accommodate the effect of socio-demographic attributes of households and individuals in a very limited fashion, which limits the activity of the method to evaluate travel impacts of long term socio-demographic characteristics of the individuals who actually make the activity travel choices and the travel service characteristics of the surrounding environment. So, the activity based models are better equipped to forecast the longer term changes in travel demand in response composition and the travel environment of urban areas. Also, using activity based models, the impact of policies can be assessed by predicting individual level behavioral responses instead of employing trip based statistical averages that are aggregated over defined demographic segments.

The future travel target behavioural consumption

Why senior age will be main travelling target.

In the past, Germany government had established tourism survey analysis to analyze survey data in order to arrive at reliable conclusions on future trends in travel behavior. To aim to find how demographic change will influence the tourism market and how the industry can adapt to those changes. The travel analysis provided data on tourism consumer behavior, including attitudes, motives and intentions. Since, 1970 year, it is based on a random sample, representative for the population in private households aged 14 years or older. Then, a continuous high scientific standard combined with a national and international users makes the travel analysis a useful tool and reliable source for tourism industry and policy decisions. It aimed to gather statistical data. e.g. on the age structure and on demographic trends, quantitative and qualitative analysis with time series data from the travel analysis. It shows e.g. not only the future volume , quite different from today's seniors, or how who will travel of family holidays will change, e.g. single parents of low, but grandparents of growing significance for tourism.

Demographic change is said to be one of the important drivers for new trends in consumer traveling change behavior in most European countries (e.g. Lind 2001). Because the growing number of senior citizens in the European Union and other industralised countries, such as the USA and Japan, looks to become one of the major marketing challenges for the tourism industry. United Nations statistics predict that the share of people being 60 age or older will grow dramatically in the coming future, and is expected to rise from 10 percent of the world population in 2000 year to more than 20 percent in 2050 year (United Nations Population Division, 2001). From its statistic, some data showed that travel propensity increased throughout life until the age of about 50 years of age and was then kept stable until very late in life 75 age. The most important results is that the travel propensity when getting older is not going down between 65 and 75 age of course, the overall development of this variable is influenced by a lot of other factors which are rsponsible for quite a variation over time. It is now possible to suggest that the general pattern of travel propensity is one of the key indicators for holiday life cycle travel behaviour, includes three stages. The growth stage tends to increase from early aduithood until 45 age old or when reaching some 80%. The next stage is stabilisation from the ages of around 50 age,until 75 age old, starting with a lower increase. Finally, the decrease stage is a slight decrease occurs once people reach the more advanced age of 75 age to 85 age old (Lohmann & Danielsson 2001).

So, it seems Germany government tourism prediction to future travellers' behaviour indicated these findings, such as on how future senior generations will travel, who had used survey data to examine the patterns of travel behaviour of a generation getting older and applied the findings to draw conclusions on the future. Also, it predicted that on the future of family trips, family semgmentation will be the travel behaviour patterns in the future. These findings together with the statistical data on demographic change allowed for a better understanding of the coming tends in family holidays. It's aim developed in consumer behaviour related to demographic change and predicted what will happen future of tourism one had to consider other influences and drivers as well, for example, trends on the supply side. e.g. low cost airlines or in travelling consumption behaviour in general whether how the past may provide a key to predict travel patterns of senior sitizens to the future.

Given the projected growth of the senior citizens market, designing specific marketing strategies to meet the prospective needs of elderly tourists will become increasingly important. It has been an implict assumption that it will be a close relationship between the travel behaviour of today's senior citizens and the those of future ones. The growing number of senior citizens in the world. e.g. China, Hong Kong, Japan, USA etc. countries. Global senior citizen tourism market will be based solely on demographic predictions about the future of the population's age structure. However, many of these seniors won't only live longer but will be fitter and more active until later in life. Many of the will also have plenty in life. Many of them will also have plenty of time and money to spend on travel. So, will these new seniors behave like today's senior citizens? Will they adopt the same travel behaviour as the previous generation or become a new market of oldies for the leisure and tourism indudtry? However, to determine the actual number of senior citizens who will be travelling and to sought to evaluate and specify certain difficult to predict the actual numbers of senior citizen to any country. However, they can be based on the implicit assumption that there is a close relationship between the travel behaviour of past, present and future seniors. But is this a valid assumption? As the reiseanalyse travel analysis survey, which was conducted in Germany every year, offered some interesting data possibiltieis. It was designed to monitor the holiday travel behaviour, opinions and attitudes of Germans and has been carried out since 1970 year, questions in the questionnaire. Data are based on face to face interviews, with a representative sample of more than 7,500 repondents, the interviews being carried out in January each year. All results refer to the average for the defined generated, which ranges generally over ten years. The group of people then at the age of 60 to 69 age is described. This corresponds to the same generation ten years ago, when they had an age of 50 to 59 age. When this methodological approach is not necessarily very sophisticated, it does have the important advantages of being cost effective.

●

How to psychological method to predict travel behavioural consumption.

On the psychological view point, I think individual traveler's character will have those kind of personal characteristics. First, simplicity searchers value above everything ease not transparency in their travel planning and holiday making, and are willing to avoid having to go through extensive research. Second, cultural purists use their travel as an opportunity to immerse themselves in an unfamiliar looking to break themselves entirely from their home lives and engage. Sincerely with a different way of living. Third, social capital seekers understand that to be well travelled is a personal quality, and their choices are shaped by their desire to take maximum of social reward from their travel. They will exploit the potential of digital media to enrich and inform their experiences, and structure their adventures always keeping in mind they are being watched by online audiences. Finally, reward hunters seek a return on the investment who make in their busy , high-achieving lives. Linked in part to the growing trend of wellness, including both physical and mental self improvement who seek truly extraordinary and often indulgent or luxurious' must have experiences.

Why needs to know the personal character of individual traveler's characteristics. Because if travel agents could feel which kinds of individual traveler's character, then who can predict which kind of travel package to design to them more easily. For example, how to determine future travel behaviour from past travel experience and perceptions of risk and safety? We need to concern that the influences of past international travel experience, types of risk associated with international travel and the overall degree of safety feeling during international travel on individual's travelling experiences likelihood of travelling to various geographic regions on their next international vacation trip or avoidance of those regions, due to perceived risk. Because individual traveler's experience of safety risk degree to the countries, it will influence who chooses to go to the countries/country to travel again.

Why travellers avoid certain destinations are as relevant decision making as why who choose to go to the country(countries) to travel. Perceptions of risk and safety and travel experiences are likely to influence travel decisions; efforts to predict future travel behaviour can benefit to individual tourist's decision making. As Weber & Bottom (1989) defined risky decision is as "choices among alternatives that can be described by prodability distributions over possible outcomes" (p.114). Some psychologists judge subjective perceptions of physical reality, i.e. image of a particular tourist destination, whereas value judgement refers to the way individual rank destinations according to whose attributes. i.e. attractiveness, safety, risk etc. factors to form on overall image. So, if the individual traveler had unhappy and worried and unsafe experiences to go to where the place(country) to travel during whose vacation time before. Then, this negative travel experience will influence who is afraid to go to the place (country) to travel again. Risk of place, country, destination or region means the danger is relatively high to the place, ie. increasing in airplane accidents, crime or terrorist activity targeting citizens of potential traveler's nationality or the probability of occurrence is great , ie. recent occurrences involving travel regions/destinations under consideration or effective actions to control consequences exist. i.e. selecting safe regions and destinations, taking extra precautions when traveling to risky destinations.

These risk factors will influence the individual traveler who chooses to cancel travel plan to go to the country again.

Another interesting research, how to predict behavioural intention of choosing a travel destination, which has focus of toursm research for years, but the complex decision making process leading to the choice of a travel destination has not been well researched. The planned behaviour model using its core constructs, attitude, subjective norm and perceived behavioural control, with the addition of the past behavioural variable on behavioural intention of choosing a travel destination.

Understanding why people travel and what factors influence their behavioural intention of choosing a travel destination is beneficial to tourism planning and marketing. Understanding travel motivation is the push and pull model. The idea of the push and pull model is the decomposition of an individual's choice of a travel destination into two forces. The first force is the push factor that pushes an indvidual away home and attempts to develop a general desire to go somewhere else, without specifying where that may be. The second force is the pull factor, that pulls on individual toward a destination, due to a region specific travel location or perceived attractiveness of a destination. The respective push and pull factors illustrate that people travel because who are pushed by their internal motives and pulled by external forces of a destination. Nevertheless, how push and pull factors guide people's attitude and how these attributes lead to behavioural intentions of choosing a travel destination have rarely been investigated. The decision making process leading to the choice of a travel destination is a very complex process. The planned behaviour model is as a research framework to predict the behavioural intention of choosing a travel destination. The model based on the three constructs of attitude, subjective norm, and perceived behavioural control (Fishbein & Ajzen, 1975).

In conclusion, the factors can influence travelers who decide to choose to travel the country, which include personal safety was perceived to the highest motivation factors among the important factors which include, scenic beauty, cultural interests, friendliness of local people, price of trip, services in hotels and restaurants, quality and variety of food and shopping facilities and services. The factors include both push and pull. Push factors include knowledge, prestige, and enhancement of human relationship etc., whereas, the most significant pull factors include high technologic image, expenditure and accessibility etc. For example, Japanese travelers visiting Hong Kong. Push factors are such as exploration dream fulfillment and pull factors are such as benefits sought, attractions and good climate city. It will be the factor of future travel patterns and motivations of sub-cultural and ethic groups for Japanese choice to go to Hong Kong travelling.

Bibliography

Backman, K., Backman, S., Uysal, M. And Sunshine, K. (1995). Event Tourism : An Examination Of Motivations And Activities. Festival Management And Event Tourism, 3(1), 15-24.

Fishbein, M., & Ajzen, Z. (1975). Belief, Attitude, Intention And Behaviour: An Introduction To Theory And Research, Boston: Addison Wesley.

Hsu, C.H.C., Cai , L.A., Li, M(2010). Expectation,
Motivation And Attitude: A Tourist Behavioral
Model. Journal Of Travel Research, 49(3),
282-296. http://dx.doi, org/10.1177/004728750
9349266.

ICT Information And Communication Technology Switzerland, 2005. ICT Fakten (ICT facts).
Available   from   http://www.ictswitzerland.ch/de/ict%2fakten/ factsfigures.asp(retrieved Dec.12, 2005) in German.

Lind, (2001): Befolkningen, Familjen, Livscykeln- Och Ekonomisk Tillvaxt. Institutet For Tillvaxtpo-litiska studier/Vinnova/Nutek.

Lohmann, Martin (2001): The 31 st. Reiseanalyse-RA 2001. Tourism: vol. 49, no.1/2001;pp.65-67, Zagreb.

United Nations Population Division (2001). World Population Prospects: The 2000 year Revision, New York.

Weber E.U., & W, P.Bottom (1989). "Axiomatic
Measures Of Perceived Risk: Some Tests And extensions." journal of behavioral decision making, 2 (2): 113-31.

THREE

SCHOOL EDUCATION MARKET

What are the factors which can influence the final grades of academic students ? I shall indicate as below:

● Tutoring method factor

The tutoring method factor includes self-determined tutoring, academic advisor schedules tutoring, group tutoring, one-to-one tutoring, peer tutoring and professional tutoring. These different kinds of tutoring method can influence the final grades to any academic student. As the cognitive learning theory and humanistic theory both are for this study conceptual framework. The results of a one-way analysis of variance determined there were significant differences in final grades of students who received group tutoring compared to one-to-one tutoring and peer tutoring compared to professional tutoring.

In fact, many colleges and universities have had to provide tutoring to attend to the needs of all students' aims to teach them how to write assignments and how to exam to get higher grades. However, any methods of a tutoring will have benefits and weakness to any students. For example, students who attend group tutoring may have an advantage because other students may contribute additional information relevant to questions, whereas one-to-one tutoring will give the students the undivided attention of the tutor. In addition, students who attend tutoring provided by their peers rather than professional tutors may feel more relaxed and relate to them differently then professional helpers. What methods do tutors use? Tutoring methods usually include self-determined, academic advisor, determined programs group, one-to-one, peer and professional tutoring. What is the relationship between final grades and tutoring programs. I suggested that academic programs, particularly professional tutoring are successful and may lead to increase student persistence in course completion. In fact, students who activity participated in the tutoring program had greater academic success compared to those who did not participate in the tutoring program. Further, no researchers had compared outcomes for students who received tutoring in a group setting rather than one-to-one settings.

In addition, no researchers had compared outcomes for students who receive tutoring from peer tutors rather than professional tutors. Also no research was found that outcomes were for students who were required to participate in tutoring services, but allowed to self-determine that schedules. However, research has shown that students who voluntary received tutoring service regularly most often received a passing grade in the course for which who received tutoring.

● Reading habits among students and its effect on academic performance factor

Reading habits are well planned of study which has attained a form of consistency on the part of students towards understanding academic subjects and passing at examinations. Both reading and academic achievements are interrelated and dependent on each other. Reading habits involve personal investigation, self-study, self thinking and analysis to each bok's content. So, reading habit is the student himself/herself motivation, it is not motivated by teachers, who need to spend their leisure time in reading both English and literature. However, the problem most students have that contributes to their poor performance in tests and examinations is lack of proper reading habits. For an excellent performance, there is the need to the student to form good reading and study habits. Whether what are the reading habits among students? Has reading habit effect on academic performance? Is there a relationship between student's reading habits and academic performance? What kind of materials to students read when who visit the library? Why do students engage in reading? People read for different reasons and purposes, some of which include for pleasure, leisure, relaxation and for knowledge.

In student view point, reading is an essential tool for knowledge transfer and the habit of reading is academic activity that increases skills in reading strategies. It seems reading habit can help any student to raise knowledge and writing ability to prepare to write their assignments for those different subjects and examinations. It is possible that examination grades and study habit has close relationship.

● Class attendance and academic performance factor

The major reasons are given by students for non-attendance which include external influences of assessment pressures, poor delivery of lecturers, timing of lectures and work commitments and financial constraints. Indeed, web-based learning approaches have become popular instead of some classroom attendance universities in our societies. So, it causes students who don't need to attend to classroom regularly. Although, some existing evidence points to a strong correlation between attendance and academic performance, no effect of the studies citied above demonstrate a causal affect. However, the levels of motivation, intelligence, prior learning and time-management skills is a major limiting factor to the utility of causal affect. However, these relationships are contingent upon a number of factors, such that it is nearly impossible to predict academic performance using socio-economic. To conclude, the non-attendance or attendance factor influences academic performance is difficult to measure, such as student motivation, socio-economic status and attendance is required to influence why the student choose to attend or not attend the classrooms.

The conclusion to drawn from this study is that gender, age, learning preference and entry qualifications did not cause any significant variation in the academic performance of students. Although, some students' academic performance were not significantly different from the rest of the students. It seems some talent students who don't need to attend any classrooms and their non-attendance behaviors won't influence their academic performance to be bad. Otherwise, some foolish students who need to attend classrooms to achieve passing grades.

● Drinking and academic motivation factor

Whether academic motivation can be a mediator for achievement. It was hypothesized that heavy drinking decreases academic motivation, which subsequently also decreases academic achievement. The effects of drinking on univerity grades: Does academic motivation play a role? However, academic achievement can be influenced by a number of factors and the effect of alcohol consumption on achievement has been of particular interest to researcher. Heavy drinking habit of students, e.g. weekly drinking alcohol, and/or consumption six or more alcohol on each occasion of drinking, these heavy drinking alcohol behaviour can influence these drinking wine students whose grades to be gone down in possible. High drinking wine or alcohol habit can cause day time sleepiness, unhealthy behaviours, like unhealthy sleep patterns because they may be linked to behavioural consequences. Due to students who regularly drink alchohol, then whose drinking behaviours have interrupted sleep cycles: They go to bed late, wake up late and experience increased daytime sleepiness. All factors of which were found to be associated with decreased academic performance. It seems heavy drinking alcohol habit of intelligent students will get the bad academic performance also.

● The link between sleep quantity and academic performance factor

Whether has it close relationship to link unhealthy sleep habits and academic performance. Such as current study examined the relationship between grade point average (GPA) and sleep, in terms of quality and quantity. In general, human need have four different aspects of sleep quantity. These aspect included number of nights spent with less than five hours of sleep during the past week, as well as during an average week, number of hours of sleep obtained in an average night, as well as the number of all nighter's the students. Results indicated a significant positive correlation between amount of sleep per night with GPA, and a significant negative correlation between average number of day per week that students obtained less than five hours of sleep and GPA.

Health sleep habits can defined , such as self-rated satisfaction with sleep, enough sleeping during the night non difficulty sleeping at night and non over sleeping. If students are unsatisfied with their quality of sleep, who will encounter studying problems, due to who lack nervous to attend any classrooms to listen any lecturers' speaking to remember any important contents of their different subjects every day. So, their non sleeping bad behaviour which will cause them to get the bad academic performance in possible finally.

● The relationship between physical fitness and academic performance factor

Whether can lacking enough physical fitness sport cause students to get bad academic performance? In fact, human needs health physical ftness of life to carrying on working or studying. Physical movements of the body are vital for normal brain development to children or young adult. So if the child or young adult chooses to spend whose time to often play video games to watch television or occupies himself/herself on the computer on the weekends and after school, instead of any physical fitness sports in whose relax time to spend time to do. It will have chance to cause blood pressure, depression and other diseases to him or her. It seems any student ought have enough time to do physical fitness to keep him or her mental health benefit to prepare to have health body to learn. Otherwise, lacking physical activity will cause lower levels of self-esteem and lower levels of anxiety to cause lower academic performance in the classroom to any students. For example, the mathematics and science students who need have health body to go to classroom to study. So, enough physical sports activities are important to these students. Due to a more focused mindset on academic performance has hindered the quality and quantity of these mathematics and science students to learn in classroom everyday. So, physical fitness has close relationship to academic performance.

● The relationship between student's learning style and academic performance factor

The student's personal factor, such as level of motivation, persistence, responsibility and need for structure, whether these factors can can influence whose academic performance. Which is learning style? It is the way a person processes, internalizes and studies new and challenging material. Student's performance may be related to learning preferences or styles as learners. Some experiments indicates that college students taught in their preferred learning styles scores higher on tests, fact knowledge, attitude and efficiency than those taught in instructional style. So mismatch of teaching styles and learning styles could give negative impaxt to students. In the psychological view, due to students tend to be bored on inattentive in class, do poorly on tests, get discouraged about the course and may conclude that who are not good in the subject. As a result, students' success in classes may depend an understanding the learning style characteristics of students who enrol in the respective courses.

● The relationship between time management and academic performance factor

Managing time is any student's responsibilities. Time management is a skill that every student should not only know, but also apply. A lot of university students complain about running out of time when who need to do a certain assignment or prepare examination. They get frustrated beause who are not able to finish it before the due date. On the other hand, they spend a lot of time to meet their friends or playing, so who have no enough time to enhance their learning of productivity in order to get low grades. For example, a subject assignment needs have a important due date to finish to submit because who lack time management skill to predict the size of assignment, who need how long time to finish. So they won't have enough time to finish the assignment to submit before the due date to cause to get fail grade of the assignment.

In conclusion, any university students ought need to considerate these bad behaviours can influence their final grades. So, you ought to avoid to do these bad behaviours to reduce your bad grades risk occurrence.

Chapter 4
OUTSOURCING SERVICE
●

Information Technology Outsourcing

In any organization information technology department, information system operations remain the predominant function outsourced, other functions are also being performed by external service providers and the relationship is between outsourcing and certain demographics: size, industry is formation intensity. The results suggest that system operations remain being performed by external service providers. Further, industry and information intensity has some influence on the extent of outsourcing of certain functions.

The first reason is cost reduction, trying to remain competitive and up-to-date is becoming a financial burden to many organizations. This is true particularly in fields, such as banking and financial services, health care and manufacturing. Hiring outsiders to handle part or even all of its information system often helps an organization to provide better services and maintain a competitive advantage. The information technology industry choice of outsourcing factor is related to size, industry type and information technology.

The second reason is technological and/or human resources in the management of the information technology infrastructure skill improvement. The information technology department outsourcing service to external service provider, includes the degree of internalization of technological resources and the degree of internalization of human resources. Some economists defined internalization of outsourcing service is as ownership is by the focal organization which takes on full control with profit and loss responsibility. Also who define outsourcing is as involving a significant use of resources, either technological and/or human resources, external to the organizational hierarchy in the management of the information technology infrastructure. So the information technology external service providers includes: applications development and maintenance, systems operations, networks/telecommunications management and user computing support, system planning and management purchase of application software, but excludes business consulting services, after-sale vendor services and the lease of telephone lines etc. outsourcing services.

The third reason is economics of scale in areas of hardware, software. This pressure is seen as the most significant factor driving today's corporate interest. An outsourcing service provision might be in a position to exploit economics of scale in areas of hardware, software and staff since it pools different kind of technological projects from many service receivers. Outsourcing information technological service can reduce the corporate's cost with the high level of IT investment, there are increasing pressures to move away from fixed expenditure, corporate overhead towards a more direct variable cost approach to control the IT operations. The IT costs can become predictable for overruns is often placed on the service provider. Outsourcing service can allow the service to gain immediate access to competitiveness in delivering products or services as well as to avoid of obsolescence risk, due to the changes in the nature of the IT infrastructure, the risk of obsolescence is high. Outsourcing can allow the service provider has the ability to diversify these risks across a broad range of service receivers. However, long term contracts might in spread the risk, the weakness is back to the receiver.

It seems outsourcing IT service has also these disadvantages: such as, loss of flexibility or managerial control. Outsourcing reduces real or perceived control over both quality real or perceived control over both the quality of software and the timetable of project since the work is now being carried out by people not under direct supervision. It also threats to long term career prospects to information system professionals because many of them do not find suitable. Is jobs or promising career paths in both areas of the corporation. Outsourcing also increases coordination cost. It may requires increasing time to communicate and coordinate with the service provider. Traditionally, the formal meeting cost of negotiating and monitoring the outsourcing contract are potentially wide ranging, indirect and substantial increasing, such as, additional releasing or transferring employees, in license transfer by software vendors and in re-negotiating contracts costs. So, the IT industry of profit motivates service provider might not be in the least interests of the outsourcing service receivers. Some IT service providers are in the business of maximizing their profit at any cost, this could run counter to a service receiver's interest.

●

Outsourcing or insourcing in human resource supply chain factor

To choosing of outsourcing or insourcing in human resource supply chain factor of the controlling service demanders needs to concern this issues: Should human resource activities be provided in house or should all or past of those activities be outsourced? The relationship between organizational structure and the HR function is an important variable. The individual activities that comprise HR systems include not only the employee life cycle from recruiting to termination, but also planning for organizational staffing needs and improving organizational effectiveness. How organizations need to outsource HR function to not care employees knowledge and skill is a factor to influence any organizations choose to outsourcing non core employees when which have no any right employees to be promoted to do the position. For example, firms engage in HR outsourcing to reduce management access HR expertise, achieve workforce flexibility, focus managerial resources and keep up with changing workplace negotiations. Also, supporting the tend is the availability of common technology platform, which can reduce costs for organizations and risks. However, organizations are afraid of losing some control over delivery of outsourcing services and finding themselves dependent on the vendor or liable for the vendors actions where there are both benefits and challenges may be informed by the structure of the relationship between client firms and these organizations offering the outsourced activities to client firms.

What variables are impacted by HR outsourcing of staffing? Which include: administrative costs for labor expense, client firm to HR relations, HR regulatory competency requirement, knowledge of cost factors, e.g. billing and pay rates, vendor markups and margins, vendor management competency requirement, client and vendor relationship, communication is between client managers and staffing vendor, employee data-available, data quality control, data security, match with job requirement, employee quality, inter-vendor competition, mining of client talent by vendor , quality content for preferred staffing vendor, standardization of business process (intra-company), strategic focus of client firm, demands on client managers vendor competency and external economic environmental viability.

However, it has dynamic relationship between the client firms and staffing vendors. Moreover, the models of human resource supply chain, every has different set of advantages and disadvantages for the client firms. The models can be relate to the decision making process on outsourcing of human resources. As strategic services tactic decisions have an important impact or selecting the particular HR outsourcing model that a client firm adopter. The another model is the balance of power and control over managing the control workers differ to decide what every worker individual skills or abilities outsourcing demand. Moreover, local contracting is also the predominant traditional model for outsourcing staffing with non-core employees. A client firm usually uses several staffing vendors to meet temporary staffing needs for seasonal functions, employee absences and special projects. The advantages of local contracting are high touch and high quality of service by staffing vendors, minimal bureaucracy, empowerment of hiring any high qualified employees to get the job done, and a relatively better fit between specific staffing vendors and functional needs.

The disadvantages of local contracting can increase costs from non-standardization of hiring practices and procedures across the client form, a significant amount of word of mouth and subjective quality issues, high local costs and client firm us subjected to the capabilities of the staffing vendors and contract employees. However, local HR contracting is the most flexible, high quality, but expense, inefficient and ineffective HR outsourcing model for the client firm. Another model is the working period to be decided to outsource HR contracting. In this situation, in the short term and on a day-to-day basis, the client firm aims to achieve on economy of scale with its staffing vendors. The total costs of temporary workers as well as internal costs for contracting with several different vendors are higher than if it needs one staffing vendors to meet all its needs. So, the client company can set the reasonable pricing that it pays for its temporary outsourcing staffs. Each staffing vendor secures a different rate range with each vendor as opposed as one contact. In the long term, it is benefiting, each specialized staffing vendor is able to fully work with each function needs temporary utilization is better than the average. Mismatches are fewer. Functional departments are able to receive a high quality / high touch service in any time period. Another model is the centralizing is when the department standardizes the staffing process to drive costs down of temporary workers. This tends to occur when a percentage of non-core employees reach a certain ratio of core employees. The advantages include more uniform standards in hiring process, billing rates and pay rates, departmental hiring managers can refocus their effort to choose outsourcing staffing, criteria may be established for a performed suppliers list and greater security for the staffing established vendors that offer higher quality services. The disadvantages include new departmental responsibilities in HR which decreases outsourcing efficiencies for the organizations daily administrative direction is rather than long term strategic direction. Usually lacking qualifications to fulfill the responsibilities, overall, centralizing of HR outsourcing is that firms can achieve more standardization which additional bureaucratic costs and the necessary non-core jobs do not get done as a need. Another model is purchasing HR, which manages staffing vendors from HR to the purchasing unit of an organizations. The goal is to continue cost reductions by increasing efficiencies. In conclusion, the main benefits of HR outsourcing include maintaining organizational control over the hiring process, application of purchasing capabilities for greater standardization in hiring processes pay rates and bill rates. So, any outsoucred HR organizations may be reduce hiring process cost.

●

Global outsourcing source strategy
in a value supply chain

What is global outsourcing source strategy in a departmental role? In a highly competitive global environment, many manufacturers are responded by setting and outsourcing relations for components and finished products with lower cost producers on a contractual electronic commerce department, (original equipment manufacturer basis). Outsourcing strategy is part of the value supply chain of corporate activated. Nowadays, global outsourcing increases organizational and technological capacity of firms and cooperating a network of remotely located external suppliers performing. These understanding the important roles that product designers, engineers and production managers and purchasing manager etc. play in global sourcing strategy empowerment. Specially, electronic commerce is popular to supply chain. For example, Toyota car manufacturing company, owns unique capabilities by designing and manufacturing certain car components in-house , i.e. insourcing. Toyota also outsource manufacturing activities, Toyota adopts purchasing necessary, but no strategic inputs from independent component suppliers on obtaining a lower cost for these inputs. For example, products would be belts, tires and batteries to vehicle products that are not customized and do not differentiate its products from its competitors. Toyota's outsourcing strategy is car strategic inputs provide differentiation, e.g. engine, transmission etc. are sources from suppliers based on strategic partnership to gain to access to suppliers' capabilities and it is also a conceptualize global outsourcing sourcing strategy to Toyota car manufacturing company.

How value chain outsourcing affects firm level performance. Global outsourcing strategy means to identify which production units that will serve which particular markets and how components will be supplied for production and thus included a number of basic choices, companies can make in decision how to serve various markets. Either choice relates to the use of inputs, assembly or production within the country to serve a foreign market or decides to use of internal or external supplies of components or finished products. In this outsourcing source input situation, the term sourcing is needed to describe how multi-national companies mange in of components and finished products in serving foreign and domestic markets. Sourcing decision making is both contractual point of view, the sourcing of major components and products are occurred by multi-national companies. First is from parents or their foreign subsidiaries. Second is from independent suppliers on a contractual basis. The first type of sourcing is known as insourcing. Otherwise, the second type of sourcing is referred to outsourcing. How to achieve economies of scale by outsourcing or insourcing sourcing input strategy? Therefore, the two outsourcing strategies are multi-faceted and require careful examination.

•

Outsourcing benefits in economic view

The two economists (Abrahamson & Rosenkopf, 1993) indicated that In long term, outsourcing can help to reduce fixed investment in finance view point, in-house manufacturing facilities and thus lower the breakeven point, which subsequently helps boost an outsourcing company whose return on equity (ROE). Thus, if any one corporate performance is evaluated on the basis of its contribution to the company's ROE. Also, in the short term or long term on resource inputs outsourcing view, early adopters of outsourcing strategy indeed experienced efficiency gains as they were able to reduce fixed investment in in-house manufacturing facilities and lows their ROE. But, later adopters may have different to gain institutions legitimacy or because of competition pressures in the industry, despite some inherent uncertainties about the long term costs and benefits of outsourcing strategy. It seems that outsourcing strategy was devised as any organization's policy makers to access trade linkages of benefits for short term or long term. Outsourcing strategy is a systematic analysis of the economic, political and regulatory implications indicates potential benefits along with a number of potentially negative side effects to any organizations. Then, outsourcing strategy will be caused this question: How to assess the risks and benefits of outsourcing for organizational sectors and nations both? The decision to change outsourcing behavior to carry a business activity may have profound implications for outsourcer and outsource receiver both, but little impact of the sector level. The common occurrence of industry decisions to outsource most manufacturing, including sale of factories, it created a new sub-sector, contract manufacturing. Otherwise, at a national level and public sectors become less distinct to outsourcing strategy. Public policy on outsourcing has stimulated extensive debate, privatization social justice and value for money etc. challenges.

●

What motivate outsourcing what is being outsourced risk and concerns?

Whether what motivate outsourcing, evidence of what is being outsourced risk and concerns? Outsourcing activities include: outsources manufacturing components and other value adding activities. Some focused on employment is outsourced another firm's employees carrying out tasks previously performed one's own employees. Outsourcing is an activity outside the organization's chosen core competencies. It seems outsourcing is a sub-contracting relationships between firms, all foreign production, hiring of workers in non-traditional jobs, such as control workers and temporary and part time workers.

What are the motivations for outsourcing reasons? Why outsourcing is needed to any organization. For example, it can enable firms to focus on core activities. The concept of focus originates in operation on a small, manageable, number of tasks at which the operation becomes excellent to specific technologies and as a risk of vertical integration advantages. Other benefits of outsourcing appear is literature on strategic management, operations management, purchasing and supply and innovations. Moreover, outsourcing can improve flexibility to meet changing business conditions, demands for products, services and technologies by creating smaller and more flexible clear evidence includes improved creditability image, greater workforce flexibility and avoiding being backed into specific assets and technologies are harder to measure. How outsourcing can improve company performance. For airline manufacturing industry example, Hill & Jones (1995) showed that the manufacture of a large portion of the Boeing 767 is Boeing's third largest commercial aircraft, which is outsourced to Japanese manufacturers, which include Fuji, Kawasaki and Mitsubish. As a result, only 10% of the value of the 767 Boeing is produced in-house. So, outsourcing is an attempt to enhance manufacturing air place industry competitiveness.

●

How can choose smarter outsourcing?

How can choose smarter outsourcing? Organizations hope to do sight options to save money, among themselves staff layoffs and a reduction of overhead costs, such as office space. Private companies have long outsourced in order to save time and money. During periods of economic growth, many organizations began to use outsourcing more frequently and staff workloads grew in proportion to increase budgets. Tasks such as conducting needs assessments, reviewing proposals, conducting site visits, monitoring and creating evaluations systems were increasingly given to outside contractors, consulting firms and independent consultants in the belief that external specialists could do the work more efficiently and effectively than company itself.

Nowadays, there is a growing stream of organizations need to research into the outsourcing of innovation activities within the innovation, management, marketing and economics disciplines. These organizations need to understand how with the outsourcing practice becoming more commonplace in their industry. However, their behaviors bring these two questions: Whether outsource or internalize innovation activities and the performance implications of this decision can support for both transaction cost and resource based arguments is examined with both theory bases showing substantial attention? Whether outsourcing innovation activities can lead to faster product development and cost savings? On advantages hand, it is possible that outsourcing may lead to higher costs and slower new product development. Further the technological uncertainty may have conflicting impacts on the outsourcing decision that are not yet well understand. When outsourcing product development has reduced costs and has proved speed to market. On disadvantages hand, outsourcing has also reduce product development time delays and higher quality concerns. Why to cause performance implications of outsourced innovation activities in transaction in cost economics and the resource-based view point? When outsourcing product development has been to reduce costs and has improved speed to market, outsourcing product development is not unlike other make or buy decisions. So, make vs buy decision is similar to logistic and IT outsourcing. Internalization of product development will be preferred when transaction costs are excessive. Otherwise, the market i.e. outsourcing will be selected when transaction costs are low. Transaction costs can include adaption, safeguarding and measurement costs. Adaption costs represent efforts to adjust contract to change conditions and are a result of environmental uncertainty. When a firm may have to revise on agreement with a partner company, this facing substantial penalties, due to an unstable market environments, the firm is likely to perform this function internally. Safeguarding costs characterize the costs of an outsourcing provider acting opportunities after investments have been made in the inter-firm relationship and are the result of transaction specific investment. Measurement costs include all expenses with confirming that contracts have been fulfilled passably. The contracting firm may face substantial costs to estimate quality for contractual services. When the sum total of these transaction costs is substantial, internalization will be favored.

●

What is environmental uncertainty factor?

Environmental uncertainty refers to unanticipated changes in circumstances surrounding an exchange in market uncertain and technological uncertainty. Market uncertainty is the fluctuation and unpredictability of demand. With respect to innovation projects, market uncertainty may cause frequent changes to the development, complications and adding expense to external contracting. These changes may necessitate renegotiation or cancellation of innovation contracts, which will likely carry prohibitive penalties (a term) transaction costs. These transaction costs promote internalization under high levels of market uncertainty. Otherwise, technological uncertainty environments, selecting market governance allows firms the flexibility to end relationship should technical requirements shift. It seems that market and technological external change factor will influence to benefits to any organizations to choose outsourcing strategy. On the other side, outsourcing can bring this question: Whether the offshore outsourcing of information technology jobs choice is suitable to any IT organizations? Nowadays. The offshore outsourcing if IT jobs from the United States has been enabled by a powerful influence of global economic demographic and technological forces. In fact, many IT companies were drawn to offshoring outsourcing because of the need for programmers to fix the Y2K problem in the late 1990- year. It is shortages of US programmers. Other factors driving this phenomenon include the wage gap between the US and developing countries, e.g. China and India, advances in technology, labor availability, expanding foreign markets and foreign government incentives. The spread of the offshoring phenomenon from low skill manufacturing to high wage white collar service industry jobs reduces the country's IT jobs critics, it represents the mobility for many US workers who saw post-secondary education as the route to a higher standard of living. The offshoring outsourcing of manufacturing and service jobs from the US to lower cost foreign nations become a national issue in a very short time. The impact of offshore outsource on the information technology sector gives outsourcing potential loss of millions of jobs at all wage levels and the critical contribution is the IT sector to US productivity growth. However, decisions about the locations of manufacturing or service facilities reflect market forces key factors include the size of local markets, capital availability and costs, labor availability skill levels and cost, logistic issues, reliability and infrastructure and IT in particular relationships with research institutions. All these factors will influence the choice of offshore outsource IT jobs strategy top any organizations.

●

Whether outsourcing will bring
what kind of work skills.

Whether outsourcing will bring what kind of work skills. Many employers choose outsourcing to employ employees. This core of our work is identifying trends which will transform global society and the global marketplace. How it influences our nature of work form health care to technology, the work place and human identity. A decade ago, workers worried about jobs being outsourced overseas. Today companies, such as Odesk and Liveops can assemble teams " in the cloud" to dosales, customer support and many other tasks. It seems outsoucring can influence many high technological job of changes. Global connectivity, smart machines and new media are just some of the drivers reshaping how we thank about work, what constitutes work and the skills, we shall need to be productive contributors in the future. As computer technology in the cloud will be used popularly to society. A signal is typically a small or local innovation that has the potenial to grow in scale and geographic distribution. A signal can be a new product, a new practice, a new market strategy, a new policy or new technology, such as online cloud computing files storage service method. It is an innovative social science method to computer users. However, this new computer files storage method influences outsourcing service of needs increasing. It will have key drivers and skills areas that will be most relevant to the technological workforce of the future.

It is estimates that by 2025 year, the number of Americans over 60 age will increase by 70%. The challenge of an aging population will come. What it means to age, individuals will need to rearrange their approach to their career, family life and education to accommodate their life plan. Increasing, people will work long past 65 age in order to have adequate resources for retirement. Multiple careers will be commmplace and lifelong learning to prepare for occupational change will see major growth. To take advantage of this well experienced organizations will have to rethink the traditional career paths in organizations, creating more diversity and flexibility. As the high technological cloud computing storage method is invented. Any organizations can save their files to the central cloud computer storage system website to save or find their files from website more easily. It will reduce their computer department expenditure and staff salary. So, outsourcing computer file storage service demands will be influenced to increase to any organizations as well as organizations will reorganize their computer department job nature to shape the kinds of social, economic and political organizations which inhabit. Outsourcing is a good solve method to assist organizations to pay cheap salary to employ many retired high age workers by contract or temporary or part time method to reduce their computer department's number of employees and the retired labors only need to pay cheap salary to learn how to use internet to help whose employers to save their files to their outsourcing computer storage service provider's central computer storage system every day efficiently. So, organizations do not need to employ many computer department staffs to avoid to pay much salaries to this computer department expenditure. They can choose outsourcing to pay cheap salaries to employ many retirement labors to assist them to do simple office storage job from internet channel efficiently and effectively. Hence, internet high technological innovation can influence office outsoucing of job duties increasing.

Whether domestic outsoucing in the America, what assesses trends and effects on job quality. Nowadays, US firms' use of contractors and independent contractors and its effect on job quality and inequality. Why firms choose contract out for certain functions and assess their predictions about likely impacts on job quality, stagnant wages, growing inquality and the deterioration of job quality are among the most important challenges facing the US economy today. Although any country's domestic outsourcing , firms' use of contractors, franchises and independent contractors any one of these factors is a potentially important influence to companies reduce compensation and shift economy risk to workers. However, the domestic outsoucing takes place on a much larger scale and effects many more workers than has been recognized ranging from low wage service workers, security guards, warehouse workers and hotel housekeepers to professionals and technical workers, such as programmers, health care technicians and accountants. These tends are part of structural change in the organization of production to influence quality of jobs and the nature of employment contract after outsourcing jobs are popular. The quality of jobs include wages, benefits, employee skills and training and mobility opportunities and job security as well as inequality across jobs. Domestic outsoucing concerns these issues: such as employment and labor law, the provision of health, pension and other workplace benefits. However, any companies choose outsourcing of employment reasons include, such as that it relates how management choices to pursue value added or cost focused strategies. Contracting out is difficult to define because a large part ot economic activity has always occurred through business-to-business transactions, as captured in macro-economic input-output models. Outsoucing job employment method can influence any one labor's individual quality of jobs. Usually, international companies choose the offshoring of work in global supply chains. Until recently, the domestic counterpart outsourcing employment method has grown supply chains to domestic or regional outsoucing employment.

What factors cause domestic outsourcing and whether firm decisions about what to retain in-house and what to outsource have changes over time. Some evidence suggests that firms have responded by focusing on their core competencies and outsourcing low value added tasks as well as higher value added specialized functions. Advanced technologies have facilitated this process by allowing firms to outsource entire functions ans more easily monitor contractors as well as employees who work, leading to new forms of networked production and rise of specialized outsouring employment firms. Domestic outsoucing influences the changes of job quality, benefits, hours, workload, job stability, schedule stability and occupational safety, health, incidence of wage theft and access to training and promotions. Predictions are less clear for job requiring professional or technicial or specialized skills or those that are outsourced to large and diversified outsourced contractors. Types of outsourced contracts include: suppliers or vendors of products, such as manufacturing inputs or services, such as business services or staffs service or staffing firms, franchisees and independent contract, such as freelancers, independent contracts or non demand platform outsourced workers. It is significant restructuring of domestic manufacturing supply chains will greater reliance on suppliers and subcontractors. In addition, the potential growth of on demand outsourcing work as well as other forms of job fragmentation. It causes this question: How outsourced workers are multiple forms of income generating work to achieve economic security and how outsourcing workers can build career across jobs and over time.

Firm in every sector of the economy contract with other firms as part of their production process, as do governmental entities. The functions that are outsourced vary widely. For example: human resources ans research and development functions, building services, recycling, regulation and compliance, accounting, credit card collection, call centres, mortage and check processing, information technology and data processing, logistics and transportation, machine maintenance, cable installation, food services, food processing, parts manufacturing and assembly, laundry and housekeeping etc. outsourced jobs causes.

Whether what business impact of outsourcing will be caused? Nowadays, IT outsourcing was clearly a part of an effective management strategy that the companies felt IT outsourcing strategy can bring to achieve positive results. Information technology outsourcing providing servicers will be predicted to provide services that is expected to raise over the next five years minimum. The companies demand clients expected benefits of IT outsourcing and determined that cost reduction, increased operation, efficiency and improved IT effectiveness. What are the impacts of outsourcing to influence better long-term improvement in the business performance? It is impossible to being benefits of significant reduction and lower growth in sellings, general and administrative expense to IT outsourcing company demand clients. Also, pre-existing corporate cultures are focused on business improvement to IT outsourcing company demand clietns. In the past researches, some economists indicated that points can be used to reflect the actual numbers increase or decrease in percent. However, their prior researches shows that prior to outsourcing, the annual growth in selling, general and administration expenses of eompanies in the study was already 4.2 points lower than sector medium. Moreover, within one to two years after IT outsourcing these companies improved even most. Annual growth in selling and general administrative expenses for them was 9.9 points lower efford to assist any IT outsourcing will have selling and administrative expenses for long term. Also, almost two-third of the companies studied outperformed in increased growth in return on asset two to three years after IT outsourcing commenced. Prior to outsourcing, the annual ROA growth rate for companies in the study ws 7.5 points lower than the sector median. After outsourcing, however these companies experienced 8.6 points higher median a substantial change of 16.1 points. Also, nearly two to third of the companies studied grew earnings faster than their peers. Two to three years after IT outsourcing, companies experienced an annual rate of growth in earnings 11.8 points higher than the growth rate of the sector median. Thus, it seems IT outsourcing can assist the IT outsourcing demand clients to reduce expenditure and to raise income both as the same time. Then, it will cause these questions to IT outsourcing demand clients. Is outsourcing influencing in an economic downturn to finance sector in the short term? Is the finance sector's renewed change for outsourcing just a temporary cost-cutting measure? Will today's economic climate initiate long term financial and productivity gains? Whether what are benefits and disadvantages of outsourcing finance sector IT. I shall demonstrate why outsourcing open source software support and maintenance can be a good choice to start. Firstly when company plans to budget cuts expenditures, IT outsourcing is often the first choice. For example in 2003 year, Zurich Financial services' sprawling IT department consisted of more than 7,500 employees. After posting a record loss of 3.4 billion the year before, Zurich decided to cut down on in those staff and outsource nearly half of its IT work. Outsourcing has successfully cut costs by 45 percent and cut the number of in house IT staff by 60 percent. Here are some of the benefits that companies enjoy when they outsource information technology functions to competent, reliable vendors.

In fact, it can be too expensive to maintain, company's own information technology, especially during a recession. Fortunately, many IT functions can be easily and efficiently outsourced, positively impacting individual company's bottom line. Employee costs are much higher than just salary and benefits, keeping employees happy, productive and busy takes time, effort and money. Although, many IT staffs will be dismissed, it will increase the unemployment ratio in societies. But, moving an IT service out of house means financial organizations don't have to worry about technology refresh costs in the future. It also cuts down on human resources requirements, specialist IT service provides which can provide the newest technologies and deliver quality service more than company itself in house information provides are the most effective to develop and implement and upgrade their clients' software or the launch on a new platform, due to the expert's time is wasted on day-to-day duties for whose other IT outsourcing demand clients. However, instead of IT outsourcing service outsourced offshoring in that service sector, how economic impact to influence the outsourced offshoring country. For example, United States continues to run an international trade surplus in services. Many Americans are particularly concerned about the loss of skilled, well paid jobs in such fields as computer programming and accounting etc. positions. These jobs seemed relatively secure at a time when many manufacturing jobs were being cost to import competition. Similarly, telephone call centers, once viewed as an esonomic development opportunity in some areas, increasingly are moving low wage countries, such as India and the Philippines. Thus, offshoring raises many questions for policymakers and general public. For example, which service jobs will be affected most by import competition. What are the likely effects of service-sector offshoring on U.S.A. output, employment and our standard of living, such as America? Is offshoring really a problem that requires restrictive government actions or are other kinds of policies more appropriate to give Americans or other countries the highest possible living standard?

The term of offshoring refers to the relocation of jobs and production to a foreign country. The relocated jobs and production could be at a foreign office of the same multinational company or at a separate company located abroad. In constrast, the term outsourcing doesn't necessary imply that jobs and production are relocated to another country. The major outsourcing service jobs include human resource, accounting and information technology etc. in-house service jobs in large organizations. However, the loss of service jobs and factory production is caused by offshoring is diffuclt to measure. It is also difficult to determine the impact of offshoring on total services employment in the United States or other countries. International trade in services covers a wide range of industries and activites. For example, travel and transportation includes travel expenditures, passenger fares and frieght and port services, royalties and license fees cover transactions including patents, copyrights, trademarks and other intangible proprietary rights to use, produce or distribute products. Other private services include many of these industries, such as education, financial services insurance, telecommunications and other professional services etc. Some economists indicated that occupational employment statistics for the Unisted States provided additional evidence that past service sector offshoring had been small. About 14 million service jobs were at risk of offshoring in 2000 year, when about 96 million service jobs had a low risk of ofshoring. The decline in the at-risk service occupations from 2000 year to 2002 year was about 218,000 jobs or roughly 109,000 jobs annually, relatively small number that is consistent with the estimates of McCarthy or Zandi. In percentage terms, employment in the at risk occupations fell at a faster rate from 2000 year to 2002 year than in the low risk occupations. This faster decline is consistent with offshoring activity, although the decline is consistent with other explanations as well, such as faster of technological change in industries employing the risk occupations or greater cyclical sensitivity in these industries. Because offshoring was not the only cause of job loss in the risk occupations, the number of jobs moved offshore was undoubtedly less than 109,000 jobs annually. However, the estimates may understate the total impact because domestic companies with expanding worldwide employment may have located may of their newly created jobs abroad even when they didn't reduce their US employment. Some of those foreign jobs might provide services to US customers and potentially foreign jobs might provide service to US . Conversely, the estimates may overstate the total job loss from offshoring of the foreign outsourcing of some support jobs prevents the loss of other domestic jobs by keeping US firms competitive in world markets. For example, cost reductions from offshoring IT jobs might help a US financial services company win foreign contracts, preserving many professionals and support jobs in the US.

Lower production costs in foreign countries are a major cause of service sector offering. Although, the costs of land and other resources may be cheaper abroad, but the main difference betweeb the US and developing countries is labor costs. There is a large gap in computer programmer wages between the US and other countries. Any organizational capital includes both physical capital, such as machinery and computers and human capital , such as skills and knowledge. The cost savings is come from offshoring also might be reduced if the firm needed to pay higher transportation and telecommunication costs or management spends more time on service quality and data security. Still, the much lower levels of wages ans benefits in developing countries suggests that many services can be produced abroad at lower cost. The in-house professional relocation of labor-intensive service activities, such as legal transcription services to countries with lower labor costs is consistent with economists' basic theory of international trade, comparative advantage. So, in-house outsourced professional service will be a corporative advantage, if the country's legal profession is poor level to compare with the another country. e.g. the skill in-house the legal professional labors of the developing country, such as China is poor educational level to compare with the developed country, such as US. So, if China large organizations chose to outsource themselves in-house legal service jobs to outsource offshoring to US legal professional lawyers to do. It can bring comparative advantage to China large outsourced in-house legal service organizations, due to these China outsourced large organizations can reduce to employ to pay too much salaries to these many in-house Chinese domestic lawyers and the US outsourced legal consultants whose can give more professional legal recommendation to serve to the China large organizations.

In conclusion, although offshoring strategy can increase unemployment chance for this disadvantge. But, all of outsourcing benefits weighs are more than the offsourcing disadvantages. However, outsourcing strategy can have these benefits to the outsourced service demanders. Such as outsourcing is no longer just about cost saving, it is also a strategic tool that may power the twenty first century global economy. Moreover, outsourcing can increase productivity and competitiveness, e.g. for every 1000 jobs British Airways sends to India , the airline saves $23 million, companies can devote a portion of their outsourcing savings to helping employees make job transitions, also leader can no longer afford to view outsourcing as a business tactic, it is now essential to remain competitive. On the world stage, workers now compete globally, so individuals must continually learn more to vie successfully with their peers worldwide, the average company only spends about 20% of the value of its outsourcing contracts to manage its relationship with the outsource provider. So, in the positive view point, outsourcing strategy can bring a potential primary driver of the global economy development. Although, outsourcing can also cause the raising of domestic unemployment chance. But companies may soon be more outsourced than in sourced, signifying a fundamental reorganization that will affect employees, managers, customers and executives. Customers' choice will increase product costs will drop and workers' roles will change. Finally, the most important, the developing country will earn comparative advantage from the developed country's employers' offshoring jobs provision. Thus, the developing country's unemployment rate will be reduced, then the global economy will be kept more balance fairly.

Reference
Abrahamson, E., & Rosenkopf., (1993). Institutional and competitive bandwagons: Using mathematical
modeling and a tool to explore innovation diffusion.
    Academy of management review, 18(3), 487-517.
Hill, C.W.L. & Jones, G.R. 1995. Strategic management, An integrated approach. Boston: Houghtom Mif In.

FOUR

ECOMMERCE MULTI-LEVEL SERVICE

FIVE

INTERNET MULTI-LEVEL SERVICE MARKET

What are the differences between multi level
marketing and direct personal sale?

It seems that multi level marketing (MLM), netwrok marketing and direct sellers scheme marketing which are under the pyramid retail sales criterion. It means only third parties with no connection to the selling organizations are considered legitimate "ultimate users". Consequently, it deems the consumption of product by distributors (participants), "internal consumption" to be illegalitimate and simply a cover for fraud.

As multi level marketing or direct sellers from pyramid schemes both marketing which need individual participant or distributor who give money to buy their products to join to whose business to earn commissions. It seems the participant or distributor will be client role more than member or business partnership role. So, it seems MLM or direct sellers from pyramid schemes which main income sources are come from participants or distributors (internal clients). Rather, the key question is to determine whether the purchasers, whoever who may be actually resell or consume their products if the sales transactions are thus reveals to legitimate, as a matter of economic principle. They are also revealised to have increased social welfare. By accepting and adopting without further inquiry the "retail sales criterion", even though it is contrary to basic principles of economics and logic. Consequently, I shall indicate these above proposed test to distinguish legitimate from fraudulent enterprise of legitimacy to multi level marketing or pyramid schemes direct sellers both sale channels.

The reasons of legitimacy to multi level marketing or pyramid schemes direct sellers include which are inappropriately not just the consumer surplus flowing from, but also the profits that the parent firm earns from selling products to dustributors for their internal consumption. This error is caused by asserting that the resulting biased estimates of cash flow are sufficient to indicate that either a pyramid scheme (multi level or direct personal sale) is in progress. These both network sale channels discard all profits earned with internal consumption and because they assume, without the justificaton or validation, that all participants (distributors) in a direct selling enterprise act to as to maximize their cash income. What is the mean of relating high rate at which individuals are to direct selling is sufficient to be defrauded. It is alternative explanations for the rate at which individuals quit direct selling (the "quit rate"), and it provides no economic analysis or inquiry as to the quit rate those distributors might exhibit outside direct selling. It implies the quit rate of distributors in either direct selling or multi level (network) enterprise is pyramid scheme comparable to what one might observe in the counter-factual in which those individuals are employed as wage labour.

As the accounting theory view, pyramid multi level marketing fraud is considered of circumstances unrelated to pyramid fraud, such as calculations of distributors (participants) income whether a parent company's current cash outflows are fully funded by inflows. More direct personal sale or phyramid theme sale business calculations in this regard are biased toward finding fraud because which discard all profits earned with internal consumption and because which assume without theoretical justification or validation that all participants in a direct selling enterprise act as to maximize their cash income. Alternative explanation for the rate at which individuals quite direct selling the quit-rate and provides no economic analysis might exhibit outside direct selling. In fact, a high rate is sufficient to conclude that distributors (participants) were defrauded is apparent upon noting that there are also high quit-rates in other undeniably legitimate businesses. A direct selling (pyramid) of only a few distributors are able to build businesses that six and seven figure annual incomes is similiarly. Chief Executive officer and the distribution of salaries at many commercial entities exhibits a pyramidal form that logic would conclude that all corporations must be considered pyramid fraudsters in the labour market. Even of an economic analysis is well intentioned from direct personal sale market or pyramid enterprises in any countries. The politicies of different countries governments advocated and other misinterpretations, impose costs on consumers, producers and society at large. An objective appraisal of the costs and benefits with using test that are generated false positives represents the first step toward a meaning ful; analysis of the appropriate public policy.

This direct personal sale or pyramid direct sales scheme is concluded by providing an examination of the costs and benefits of regulation and increased enforcement. It seems direct personal sale market has no any legal doctrine support that only sales to third parties constitute legitimate business activity and application of logic and the misinterpretation and misapprehension of prior court rulings that have biased inquiries into the potential to generate false positives. So, some economists have failures of logic and economic that have characterized prior evaluations of public policy low and pyramid schemes or direct sale market.

Our goal is to providing some guiding principles to indicate economically sensible, how a true pyramid scheme or direct personal sale market can be identified and the costs and benefits of different approaches as to how fraud should be detected, with MLM and pyramid direct sale schemes. Otherwise, Multi level market, MLM compensates not only in the form of commissions on sales to distributors (participants), but it also compensate commissions on the sales of it's recurits. The fact, that the share prices of MLM enterprises that have one public have remained positive indicates that the market believes MLM enterprises have value and that this value will be sustained. In constrast, a direct personal sale market enterprise is unsustainable, e.g. a pyramid scheme that will collapse. Or always faces the threat of being shut down as a fraud by regulators, would not be able to sustain positive market value.

It is important to note that legitimate multi level network direct selling benefits not just the parent firm and distributors, but also businesses and society at large. A MLM's products may require its salespeople to invest meaningful time and effort in educating the client as to the benefits of the product, resulting in a long sales cycle before sale is concluded. MLM provides the opportunity to every participant (distributor) to build to personal networks to introduce potential purchases to products. As a matter of economic principle of revealed preference or revealed profitability.

Similarly, consumers who choose to purchase from legitimate MLM network direct sellers, they perceive more value in purchasing from a direct seller relative to other alternatives.

Many distributors join the MLM to purchase a preferred product at a lower price. Other distributors find MLM is a convenient way of support their income on their terms and according to their needs, for example by working why reasonally or part time. Another participants may find that participation in a entry point into a center or business opportunity to invest in their human capital and to acquire a network of business connections. Other participants may find that MLM (network selling) is the perfect match for their talents and skill sets. The goodwill to MLM is needed to concern. Consequently, consumer protection efforts have focused on identifying. Because, same MLM enterprises pretend to be legitimate direct sellers, such as fraudsters' debase the goodwill are trust that legitimate direct selling has established with consumers. Resultly, the direct personal sale enterprises pretend to do legitimate business activities to influence the unhealth or poor economic growth in societies. Otherwise, the Multi level market (MLM) or network market enterprises can do more legitimate business activities to influence the health or poor economic growth in societies.

However, muli level marketing, MLM is as a very popular business model in the Western countries. It is a kind of the method of distribution of products. The method of building a sales network, it is one of the safest carries a very low risks ways of conducting business activity. The enter is to any markets, it is usually with market entry barriers and huge capital needs. Lack of expansion and lack of awareness of common practices. In the traditional business model, the risk of failure is very high. Also, unknown is the uncertain concerning the return on investments. However, despite high level of risk, this is the most popular business model.

So, multi level marketing is also called "network marketing". It is one of the fastest developing and still the least understand methods if introducing products to the market. It is mainly due to poor understanding of the system that multi level marketing is often regarded as network sales, pyramid sales or even pyramid schemes. It is marketing strategy and way of functioning of a company and its partners' independent distributors. Multi level marketing is a branch of direct sale. It involves offering products and services directly to clients on the basis of individual contacts, usually at direct's home, workplace or in other locations outside permanent retail sale branches. It is a form of sale outside, a traditional ship chain. It allows sellers to build personal structures of partners, who provide additional commissions from their sales. Every seller in multi level marketing has an opportunity to build own structure of salesman in which everyone is rewarded based on the marketing plan valid for each company. At the same time, achieving higher earnings, it is as a marketing strategy, way of functioning of a company and a system allowing to build individual network for independent distributors, classifying it has a branch of direct sales is a big mistake.

What is it's differences to pyramid scheme, MLM or network market and direct personal sale method? First, MLM is a retail sale, which is the most basic form of distribution carried out by means of a retail branch, e.g. grocery shop, chemist's shop department store, online auction site. Second, direct personal sale method is covering ususally the sale of insurance, kitchen wave houses etc. products. In this model of distribution commission from sold products goes only to the seller, who can't build network of his distributors. In order to sell products or services offered by a particular company, who has to be employed in the company as a sales representative. This means that who works for the owner of a company, the company's whose employer, thus the sales representative doesn't work for whose own benefit as in case of personal direct sale marketing. Third, direct personal sale marketing is transferring a product or service from the producer of service provider to the consumer. Otherwise, MLM, Multi level marketing is as a system of rewarding people who contribute to sale of products or provision of services. In the multi level marketing method people contributing to sale are those who recommend a purchase directly from a particular company. The employee whose is provided in course of making an order is rewarded for a recommendation resulting in actual sale, as the bonus system is usually multi level and allows generating passive income, income is not the direct effect of the work of recommending person. This works, this way is as every person has the opportunity to build individual consumer distribution structurer. In order words, multi level system rewards for directly recommended persons and recommended directly by direct ones. Fourth, MLM, it means mail order sale, this kind of distribution is characterized by lack of retail points in which products could be exchanged for money. The client makes an order directly in the company after learning about its offer on television, in telephone conversation or from a received catalogue. Finally, direct personal sale method is an illegal organization of sales, which is often mistaken for muti level marketing. One of the main reasons for an illegal organization is presented as a multi level system. The difference that makes pyramids illegal and multi level making legal is the inability to distribute a product or provide service. If there are no sales of a product, it is impossible to take about marketing companies by promising high sales convince participants to pay high one off about of money that allows then to participate in the programme which makes it impossible for participants to generate sales, as all payments go to the account of those organizing the business. Thus, direct personal sale is nothing like multi level marketing or network marketing . MLM, in which sale is always based on a product or service and the commission system rewards participants depending on the contribution, regardless of held position. So, MLM, it is a network created based on contacts and ties between people and the participation of all members of the network in this activity.

●

Whether multi levelmarketing can assist economic growth.

We can view multi level marketing from two perspectives, one of them is the point of view of concept, the producer or the company for which multi level marketing is one of possible ways of introducing a new product to the market bearing huge cost with promotion and without the need to transfer rights to a product to someone. The second perspective is the point of view of an independent distribution for whom multi level marketing is a model of business which doesn't require a concept or bearing the risk with investing capital, as in case of typical business activity or franchising, such an approach makes it possible to define MLM as method of distribution of products, in which costs associated with advertising and marketing are covered at the moment of actual sale. Sales are fueled by clients of the MLM company who use their contacts to recommend the purchase of particular products. The MLM company rewards the recommending person with a commission calculated based on the company's marketing plan for a recommendation ending with actual sale. Any marketing plan creates the possibility to generate unlimited revenues and at the same time eliminate risk with the necessity to invest substantial capital required to launch typical business activity.

How Multi level marketing can assist socio-economic development. For example, insurance business is a kind of MLM business, whether it can assist socio-economic development for long term. In insurance sector, insurance companies are looking for innovative methods to spread the message and maximum business in the short time. Many local MLM companies having quite large spread in the market with leading insurance brands to promote their insurance products along with their own products. Insurance sector makes available long time debt for the economic development of the country. At the same time, the MLM route provides employment opportunities and enhances their social status. The MLM members have opportunity to develop themselves personally. This multipe rise of MLM companies can be looked at as a social contribution and these insurance MLM companies or cooperatives are as a development oriented social movement. How insurance sector can assist the economic and social impact of MLM as a tool which can influence society through employment generation, mobilzing long term funds and improving quality of life of people. There has opportunity to attractive propective candidates to gain network marketing companies. Past studies indicated the fact that a 100 % annual turnover rate among sales personnel in certain network marketing company is not unusual. According to the Direct Selling Association in th United States, it indicated 70% of the revenue from the direct selling industry was generated by network marketing companies and most of this come from the better known companies, such as Amway, was multi level instead of single level compensation plans. Such as India, network marketing was in India during mid 90 year was followed by the establishment of the Indian arm of Amway corporation The total turnover of network marketing companies in India was estimated at $30,104 rising in 2005 year with an annual growth rate of 25%.

It seems Amway can assist USA Government to earn much taxation income and sale income to reduce USA unemployment rate. As, Amway exports to India market. Indian Direct Selling Association (IDSA) facilitates membership to build network marketing companies. So, India is a good network marketing for Amway MLM company. However, consumers often have negative perceptions of direct selling organizations and network marketing organization in particular. The aggressive selling techniques, exaggeration of facts in network marketing organization recruiting and pyramiding scams together toward a basis for this negative perception. Network marketing is a subset of direct selling and is also known as multi level marketing structure marketing or multi level direct selling. Network marketing can best be described as a direct selling channel that focuses heavily on its compensation plan because the distributors (members of the networks) may receive compensation in two fundamental ways. First, sales people (distributors) may earn compensation from their personal sales of products and services to the consumers (non-member of the network). Second, they may earn compensation from sales to purchase from those persons whom who have personally sponsored or recruited into the network (down lines), these down lines continue sponsoring or recruiting to the network sharing the benefits with their sponsors or recruiters (up lines). So, the aim of MLM network market which reward sales agents for buying products and selling products and finding other agents to buy and sell products. In common, the agents (distributors) or participants can earn marketings ranges from 20% to 50% of sales income. In addition, distributors can also receive a monthly commission for their personal volume which is the value of every product who personally buy or sell. Further, the distributors also receive a net commission on the sales of those who recruit into the networks. It seems that the sales developed network marketing are not developed from sales created by retailing, but also developed through recruiting or sponsoring independent distributors. Thus, as distributors continue to recruit or sponsor not distributors to expand whose network, the new distributors will contribute new sales to the network and gain commission in return. This hunge incentive makes the investment in insurance very attractive for a member. For example, coverage margin on first premium for insurance policies can earn the range of 30% to 40%. This given the leverage for structuring the insurance sale through MLM. MLM is a marketing function in which sales people are paid for their personal contribution as well as for the persons who recruit in to the function or process. Employees or sales people who are individual team to work from which who get a reward on the achievement sale force. So, who can sense much ideas to help marketing organizations to raise high demand when demand is too high and the current employees can't meet those are recruits come in the till the position. So, employees are encouraged to bring many employees to the organization.

MLM is also a very important function in providing jobs for the jobless. The recruitment process looks for young jobless people and earns them on income from which who can support themselves. It is happy feeling to know that you are working and at the same time providing opportunities for the loss fortunate to support them. You have chance to increase your paid if you introduce someone to work as participant or recruit or distributer role to any MLM market. It will reduce the numbers of unemployment of the insurance company in society. The idea presents people with great and better learning of the MLM strategy. When people are recruited in to the business, who are trained about its functions. This training acts as a good way of future advancements in the field. It also helps those individuals to use the knowledge to their advantage once who leave to job to enter marketing or sale career.

The job presents flexibility in hours work. Due people can work at any time who feel fits in them schedule. It can also train them to learn how to achieve whose sale target and attempt to do own business and no and captial spending. Is network marketing or multi level selling marketing as it is called all about getting rich quick with minimal effort? Multi level marketing or network marketing means referring products or services directly to consumers within your network. It involves building a network. For each referral is made by the network. The preceding link or upline as those individuals are called in network marketing terms, gets a certain percentage of commission. MLM, network marketing doesn't need you to be a user of the product or service that you would eventually be referring within your network. Network marketing or MLM only need you put ability to put in lots of hard work. In fact, twice as much as in a regular job or business, willingness to learn new diversified skills, ability to discipline your ability to be as network with like minded people who can help you. So, MLM can help unemployment people to find either freelance or temporary or permanent kinds of position choices, such as sales person or distributor role in MLM company. So, network (MLM) marketing can offer various benefits to them like, lower initial costs of setting your business excellent training and product/service knowledge from industry experts, opportunity to earn additional residual income with a greater chance to move into a full time earned income model, flexibility to work at your own pace and time choice of retiring whenever you want.

Network market can be kind of multi level marketing. As network marketing is confronted with a number of issues that include the continuous erosion of campaign effectiveness, the fragmentation of traditional markets, the disappearance of the vendors' information advantage and significant changes in the distribution channel. Based on established building blocks of marketing and social network theory, a conceptual framework called network theory to integrate the two fields in a systematic way.

The networked marketing framework provides a structure for identifying the customer social network's impact on the marketing effectiveness in the different customer lifecycle phases and suggests the use of certain tools to acqire knowledge about the nature and the functional details of the social influence. However, the network marketing framework was tested in a setting on an international sample of a large company's customer database. How customer social network activity with an impact on marketing is the most intense in the purchase phase and the least. Hence, in the awareness phase, as well as the fact, that product and communication are the mix areas most impacted by social networks. For example, health care is an individual necessity and kind of national luxury product of a kind of multi level decision models. Due to health care is neither a necessity or a luxury, it is both since the income elasticity varies with the level of analysis. With insurance, individual income elasticities are typically near zero, when national health expenditure elasticities and commonly greater. It is to expected that measured income elasticities will differ for an individual, a risk-pooling group, or a national health system, just as price elasticities for individual, firm and market demand normally differ from each other. In past, some economists indicate income elasticity of individual, health expenditures under insurance (usually 60% to 95% of total spending) is typically near zero or negative, when the elasticity of national health expenditures with respect to national income is typically greater than 1.0. So, it seems individual income level and health factor has close relationship to decide to buy any health insurance policies.

Whether how multi level decision model quickly resolves to make evident the role of social and private insurance in linking micro and macro analysis in health economics. Within an insurance group, the bulk of the health resources will be allocated to those individuals who are ill and to get benefits from medical care. Individual budget constraints and ability to play concerns are pooled insurance financing. The contrast between the behaviour of the average individual, and the behaviour of the group to buy medical health insurance mean is well illustrated by insurance. However, medical health insurance pools are not only likely to display separation between group and individual behaviour, who are designed to bring about such a separation. The purpose of medical health insurance is to remove the individual budget constraint, and to reduce or eliminate the influence of cost of care on patient's and physician's decisions of how much care to use. If persons are fully insured, correlations with measures of individual income provide no information about income effects per each, e.g. the effect of monetary budget constraints, but instead reflect the influence of other unmeasured variables, cost of time, family resources, education, preferences etc. that are correlated with an individual's income. Hence, it seems that multi level model of determinants of pyramid or network sale method is suitable to sell in health insurance market. In any country's health insurance market, it will have two kind groups of people who will feel who have need to buy health medical insurance product. One group is without purchase any health medical insurance product , and another group owns health medical insurance product . At the macro level, income effects are still strong to influence anyone to decide to buy health medical insurance product, but variation factor due to differences in health status can also influence anyone to decide to buy health medical insurance product . With the country's people who feel need of health medical product, the pooling of funds will remove the insurance market income constraints and tends to strengthen the correlation of individual health status with expenditures. However, individual income effects still dominate the insurance market in the health medical insurance any country. So, it seems that health medical product insurance will have large share to lead to any country's insurance product income among of the travel insurance, accident insurance, life insurance, car insurance, employee welfare insurance etc. different kinds of insurance products market in any country. So, mulit level marketing shall be suitable to enter insurance product sale market.

Direct sale represents a modern product distribution system directly to consumer. Generally, directly to their homes, to their workplace or other places, besides retail shops. Ths best known type of direct sale, the network marketing or multi level marketing implies the existence of a network of distributors which earn income from selling on commission, to which who add the trade marketing. So, insurance, travel agent, share broker, property agent etc. these occupations which can belong to multi level or network marketing.

Following, I shall discuss the another kind of multi level marketing, e.g. franchise business. Franchise means the field of activity in which it was used. It is a license allowing the designee to sell and market a company's products or services in a particular place, using the name or the trade mark of the company, e.g. Mc Donald fast food restaurant. It allows whom to do business for the franchise owner, but not through the franchise owner. From the marketing point of view, franchise represents a distribution system based on the partnership between two parties which are legally independent. Between the franchisor (the proprietary owner, the owner of the trade mark of products and services) and the franchisee. However, developing a franchise using a well known trade mark, so it is a more complex distribution system in multi level marketing view point. Also, franchise business can be sold from internet sale channel in the multi level marketing technological view point.

●

Why the internet has positive influence on direct sale industry in multi level market to assist economic growth.

However, an important factor for increasing the turnover generated by direct sale companies and multi level marketing network represents a structure that is continuously changing. As technological changing, internet invention can raise the MLM sale method of chance. In multi level sale marketing, as house agent or franchise sale agent, insurance agent, share agent etc. these kind of occupations who can expand their businesses market from internet. Some of the trends indicate strong growth multi level products in international market. Also, high participation of women in multi level marketing, women are begining to realize that the internet makes it possible for them to reinvent themselves and begin a multi level business that requires little risk and low start up cost, such as internet sale method, these are no age limit to develop the multi level internet sale channel business and internet sale business can be an important market shares for household products in multi level marketing globally.

Besides these trends, the internet has positive influence on direct sales industry. Internet has had an impact in relations between direct seller and the company and between the direct seller and the consumer. The main multi levels through which the internet helps the development of multi level sale industry. Due to the internet has allowed direct sellers and customers to maintain contact outside the face to face meetings, it also allows direct sellers can use blogs and social media page to sell whose products, direct sellers can use electronic mailings and have online access to products and services brochures, the customers can pay to buy any online products through internet banking conveniently, more and more people were extended his professional activities of direct selling through the use of the internet and social networks, a direct selling activity can be run from home and doesn't require a high investment. Some may even give follow up orders by electronic means.

From the seller's point of view, the major attraction of direct selling is that internet sale channel offers an equal and flexible income opportunity to men and women, across all ages, level of experience and social origins. In the multi level marketing view point, the direct selling industry development trends will be direct influence by maintaining these advantages for the distributors and by using and developing the communicating modern technologies. So internet sale channel will be the potential multi level marketing to influence how to distribute products or service and to through direct sales and mulit level marketing are determined by a set of economic technological and even social factors.

Whether multi level marketing can influence economic growth in poverty countries.

I feel that the role of multi level marketing in poverty countries to influence economic growth is important. For example, some businesses who need to manufacture and sell whose products to clients directly. So who need to set up factories and to open shops in local and overseas markets. It seems who need to exploit and save many investors loading more minimal amounts to prepare to sell immediately. It will raise recruiting new downlines and high cost of products as well as who also need to establish production plants in themselves countries or foreign countries to exploit local or overseas economics and to reduce the numbers of unemployment, among many other benefits. It seems the role of multi level marketing can reduce poverty countries unemployment ratio from internet sale channel, e.g. online salesperson , delivered products service and website design technician or computer technician etc. different website related positions will be created to sell to any online buyers conveniently from online sale channel.

Multi level marketing, e.g. online sale channel method can assist any country's businessmen to sell whose products to overseas easily. So, multi level marketing is one global sale market. Such online businesses that empower the people by providing opportunities to the first time businessmen to start businesses to sell their products to overseas market from internet (online sale) channel easily in the beginning. Moreover, multi level marketing has the potential of being a good source for job creation, income generation to sell products to any countries' buyers from online sale channel by websites contact conveniently at their homes.

Whether multi level marketing can solve poverty challenge. If multi level marketing deliberately target the poor as recruits, what role does multi level marketing play in income generation? Is there any relationship between

MLM and job creation? Does multi level marketing (MLM) lead to skill and personal development of MM distributors? There are several appraches to poverty challenges. Examining them provides a necessary understanding of the nature of poverty. There are five main approaches to cause poverty challenge: The economic growth, the basic needs of rural development, the target and employment creation approaches. First, the economic growth approach would be leaded to distribution of income by the participation of the poor. In fact, economic growth need long time to develop in any countries. Also, multi level marketing, e.g. online sale channel needs a long time to build online buyer numbers to sell to different countries from distributors' websites globally. It seems this online sale method can assist global economic growth to give benefits to the developing countries to poverty people to solve unemployment challenges during any online businessmen build their websites to sell any products for long term. So, solving poverty challenge is needs long term time to develop any country's economy growth. Multi level marketing can be one of online sale method to solve unemployment challenge to poverty countries globally. Second, the rural development approach recognizes that poverty is multi dimensional. Thus, it aims at providing basic necessities of life, such as food, clean water, shelter, education, health care, and employment to rural dwellers in general. However, the limitation of this approach is that it doesn't directly target the poor. Again, decisions on rural areas to target may be done from political motives. Third, Target approach specifically aims at certain groups in the implementation of poverty programs, e.g. provision of social safety nets, micro credit and school meal programmes etc. Finally, employment creation approach emphasises the need to eliminate unemployment and underemployment. This will be achieved by creating employment from online sale channel.

The whole concept of multi level marketing is relatively new to any European and Western countries where which have existed for long term. For example, the DVD disc is a conglometrate of all firms that distribute to buyer contact in location away from fixed areas, like retail stores particularly at home. It is the locational characteristic that distinguishes it from other forms of personal selling. Multi level marketing is a subset of the DVD disc distributors are used in selling company products and also in recruiting other distributors. As a result, they receive compensation for their sales and from sales of those individuals who recruit. The senior distributors are called uplines when their recruits are called downlines.

Other common products sold through multi level marketing include health and fitness product, cosmetics, cleaning agents, electrical appliances and several others which are popular to sell from this MLM marketing either network market or/and online market both methods.

It is very important to influence many multi level marketing companies do not incur any cost on advertisement since who can use internet to advertise whose products in their websites to let global online buyers to discover after they type the seller's website address to enter their websites at home conveniently. The distributors in MLM are usually organized into networks structure connection. Two main types of such structures are the binary and unilevel structure. The former allows just two direct downlines at each level and the other direct recruits are to be placed at different levels in the network of downlines. On the other hand, the unilevel structure permits the recruitment of an unlimited number of downlines. Direct selling firms usually opt between two choices either employees or independent distributors. There are no salaries or other fixed costs associated with recruitment of independent distributors. So a non selective recruitment used with a straight method of compensation often tends to draw poverty people easily earned incomes from only a modest commitment in time and effort. It seems to commission income method. The recruitment of a new distributor allows for only a single connection. However, double registration of a single distribution is not compatible with the MLM compensation plan. A distributor is allowed to participate in three activites of the MLM company's purchase of the products as users, sale to customers and access to mark up profit and recuritment that expansion of the network occurs. The diffusion of the product or service in the market is stimulated strong by the consumption or purchase of the product.

The benefits to MLM offers to distributors include low start cost, distributors can enjoy from the income of others, e.g. the downlines benefit in the distribution network of online sale to different advertisers can help the distributor to advertise whose products to earn commission income from website; online retail group volume and other bonuses and incentives, personal development via training and business support materials to sell from online sale channel, enhanced enterpreneurial spirit to sell products from onlibe channel globally, improved interpersonal skills and increased self confidence and jobs creation from online sale channel.

Nowadays, estimate that 97% of products are purchased and use consumption, which are consistent with legitimate multi level marketing to earn commission income, e.g. a online sale channel is more than a pyramid sale channel. Many of business operations are consistent with the socially beneficial from MLM model and inconsistent with the socially harmful pyramid scheme model. Applying on economic test that requires member performance payment incentives to be primarily funded out of retail based product sales to be classified as a legitimate MLM, based on prior test, at least 62% of total life or eating product purchases would need to be retail based online sale channel. However, multi level marketing is a mulit million dollar global industry. There exists differentiating a valid mulit level marketing scheme and pyramid money circulation scheme. Multi level or network marketing is a form of business that uses independent representatives to sell products or services to family or friends etc. It is a business strategy, which involves participants at various levels, the level above getting returns at the levels below it. Basically, it works on the principle of duplication to increase retail or sale activity. The survival of the system, depends on the chain of earns commissions from retail sales who makes, and also from retail sales made by other people who recruit.

Direct selling organizations can be of various types, multi level format, network hierarchal structure or the organization can be flat. Multi level marketing activity is a method of distributing products or services in which is from distributrs. MLM has these characteristics: the presence of sponsorship lines that create financial rewards between distributors. Suppose x recruits y, x becomes y's sponsor and distributors. Suppose x immediate upline y recruits z, z who as personal recuits of y, and x are y's frontline people (z, t and u) recruited by same sponsor y and on same level and members of the same generation (z, t and u) sponsorship lines seem like family trees. In fact, these sponsors are often called genealogies. Suppose persons s and y are both recruited/sponsored by x. However, y has been more aggressive, heavily recruiting than s. y will become more financially successful than s, even through they are on the same level and had entered the business together. The higher the sales a group generates, the higher would be the amount of commission received by x. There are numerous recognition levels, for example, Amway has various levels of recognition, each with its own unique title and perks. One begins as a basic distributor, works whose way up through the ranks from silver producer to gold distributor to platinum direct distributor to Ruby direct distributors climbing up the ladder to crown direct distributor to crown ambassador direct distributor. But none of the levels and title is authoritative. In MLM schemes, the uplines are paid commissions and bonus on the sales made by their respective downline members. The company using multi level marketing method is a MLM company. The MLM company can be a firm, an individual corporation or other business entity, e.g. Amway, Mark Kay, Modicare etc. MLM entities. It's features include word of mouth sales, means savings on marketing and advertising costs, company can change their similar products in stores, the technique develops loyal customers who enjoy buying from other people who know. It is such a pyramid scheme " which concentrates on the commissions, the participant could earn just for recruiting new distributors" and which generally ignore the marketing and selling of products and services. Pyramid scheme means any sales device or plan under which a person gives consideration to another person in exhange for compensation as the right to receive compensation which is derived primarily from the introduction of other persons into the sale device or plan rather than from the sale of products or services or other property. Pyramid means a multi layered network of subscribers to be a form by subscribers enrolling one or more subscribers in order to receive any money benefits directly or indirectly, as a result of enrollment. It is similar to a continuous chain of participants or investors is recuited, in which each pays a fee to participate and receives money by recruiting others into the system. So each participant can build multi layered network of individuals to have chance to earn more benefit, if who can distribute products to sell successful from whose downline recuriters network.

Finally, the main question is whether this MLM network sale method can assist any country economic growth. I shall analyze what the difference of social effects (influences) are from these kind of sale methods, such as direct personal sale and auto online sale and multi level (network) sale. A phenomenon appears that the distribution companies accept normal direct personal selling method to cause education expenditure to bring loss their bases of values all at once. It comes a lot of direct sellers are lost to any countries. Due to it raise the compensation to the choice of direct personal sale companies. For example, China government achieves laws and policies to stop direct personal sale scheme companies to enter to local market to sell their products. Because China decides to protect its local businesses benefits to let them have ability to sell their products, due to reducing the number of growing foreign direct personal sale scheme companies exist in China itself country. Although, China will reduce GDP income from foreign direct personal import sale. But it can protect its local businessmen benefits to reduce competition. Otherwise, Multi level (network) marketing is a marketing approach that can motivate its participants to promote a certain product among their friends. It can exist in one form before in the internet age began, such as pyramid scheme. Social networks are everywhere, our email and phone address books, our famil relatives etc. Social network has web-based form, as facebook, twitter, linkedin networks made them more tangible. Moreover, internet can be good sale channel for multi level market, it gives the potential to accumulate small rewards from each participant to a sizable sum, as internet channel can allow advertisers to attract early adopters to earn commissions when the advertisers can help any multi level market companies to sell products successfully from internet channel. So, online advertisers and participants or distributors who can earn profit from multi level marketing. It seems Multi level marketing can give chance to let any participants to buid many downline recruiters to assist the team leader to sell many products from internet channel. So, the team leaders and team members do not need capital to set up their businesses and who can do business with the MLM company together easily from internet channel.

MLM or network market is often compared such as direct sales e.g. insurance, franchises etc. In fact, it is in the nature of pyramid schemes for the money to go to the person at the top of a pyramid of participants, with the majority of participants found to be in a losing position at the bottom regardless of when it collapses or is terminated. So, the compensation plan can be considered product-based pyramid schemes or recruiting MLM's because their compensation plan rewards recruiting of distributors through commission from their purchases more than selling direct to consumers. Distributors must not need to purchase products from the MLM in order to participate in the business. These findings raise some important questions: what kind of business has no clients? Only MLM's pretending to be direct sellers. Who is buying the products that can earn income from different countries residents online sale channel. Only MLM's distributors and advertisers are their main customers. If there are no direct sales to speak of, then who is making profits of these supposed sales. Only MLM company founders and officers. Whether multi level marketing can be potential tool for socio-economic development. For example, insurance business is just one among them. Selling insurance policies can operate from internet channel conveniently, traditionally is considered as a job or business. With the competition raises in industry sector, companies are looking for innovative methods to spread the message and maximum business in shorter time. Many local MLM companies have quite large spread in the market, as joining with leading insurance brands to promise life product policy protection to reduce clients' risk loss from internet MLM sale method. So, insurance sector makes online MLM route provides employment opportunities of people and enhances their social status. This multiple role of MLM companies can be looked at as a social contribution and which can develop oriented social movement.

In conclusion, MLM can raise employment generation, mobilizing long term funds and improving quality of life of people. In traditional, successful personal selling based on referrals is the key to ensure regular expansion of client base and building long term client relation. A country like India offers well run MLM online marketing networks to promote consumer products. Conveniently online MLM marketing may become slow or stagnated over a period of time. Online, Multi level marketing may be the tool in such situation, India has many people, so the online multi level businesses can be built to attempt to operate in this country. Concept selling mostly used personal selling as a tool where the sales people depend on referrals. In MLM technically, e.g. online sale, the promotion expenditures on advertisments channel margins etc. is distributed among the participants as individual product distributors or product advertisers , as who can do online business from commission incentives to build businesses from internet. Hence, internet technology can raise MLM to have competitive advantage. For example, it is common knowledge that MLM works on the concept of time leverage. A work to be done by you 100 days can be completed in one day if you have 100 people under you in a chain doing one days work. You can earn a % of incentive for the work done by each of those 100 people under your team downline. Through it is given various names like network marketing, freelance network chain marketing. To conclude, MLM can assist any countries economic growth to compare other kind of sale methods easily in the short time in possible.

SIX

MTR (UNDERGROUND TRAIN) TRANSPORTATION SERVICE

● Why MTR underground train transportation needs to know passenger behaviour

Understanding individual passenger behaviour is essential for the design MTR transportation, because who can choose to catch bus, taxi, tram, train ferry etc. different kinds of public transportation tools. Individual traveler who decides to catch which kinds of public transportation tools, it depends on whether the public transportation tool can provide real time travel information, liking link travel time schedule. So, MTR underground train needs to understand where it has terminal to give convenience to the local living areas of time travelers to choose to catch MTR easily. Although, MTR ticket fare is one factor to influence any passengers choice. But, those other factors can also influence them to choice. e.g. MTR any terminal location of convenience, short time travelling, none crowding in busy (peak) time, MTR platform waiting arrival time, none sudden MTR engineering machines broken accident events occurrence frequently etc. different factors, any one of these factors which can influence passengers who choose to catch MTR or other kinds of transportation tools.

● Why route choice can influence passenger behavioural choice

Usually, the busy time passengers will regard the route choice as a coordination problem to influence them to choose to catch which kinds of transportation tools. The route choice is as an opportunity costs to influence any busy time passengers to decide to choose to catch which kind of transportation tool which is the best right choice in the right time among of them. In the short time, for example, it seems any busy time passengers will choose to catch bus to substitute MTR underground train transportation tool, due to who feels the bus can arrive any destinations to compare other kinds of transportation tools in the most short time. However even if the MTR can either charge cheaper ticket fare to sell full day or charge discount ticket fare to sell in the busy (peak) time to compare to bus fare. It is possible that the busy time passengers will still choose to catch bus, if between the bus terminal and the another bus terminal that distance is the shorter time route to spend time to arrive destination to compare between the MTR terminal to the another MTR terminal arrival time . Also, although the busy time passengers will feel to enounter traffic jam to influence sitting or waiting bus time to be longer time in possible and who also feel MTR can avoid traffic jam problem. However, usually any busy (peak) time passengers will feel the chance of traffic jam occurrence will be less. So, the short bus route choice is more potential factor to influence the busy (peak) time passengers still to choose bus to catch.

However, if anyone wants to investigate results of day-to-day route choice which can be transferred to more realistic environment. It is necessary to explore individual behaviour in an interactive experimental set up to ensure busy (peak) time passenger transportation behavioural choice. For example, a passenger has a choice between a main road (M) and a side road (S) for travelling from (A) to (B). (M) is faster if (M) and (S) are chose by the same number of passengers. So, this method can be researched whether MTR terminal station is located at the main road (M) or the side road (S) where is more suitable to accept to passengers generally.

● Why trip time reliability and crowding factors can influence MTR passenger choice.

Other problem is MTR busy (peak) time's crowding in public transportation occurrence of MTR underground train transportation tool is becoming a growth to concern as MTR demand growth at a busy (peak) time. To capture the MTR passengers benefits with reduced crowding from improved MTR public transport service and image. It is necessary a identify the relevant dimensions of crowding that are meaningful measures of what crowding means to MTR passengers. Two main influences on MTR model choice that are growing in relevance are trip time reliability and crowding. It represents a benefit-cost framework. In fact, MTR passengers can be willing to pay more expensive ticket fare, it MTR can avoid crowding and short and the accurate arrival trip time between terminals is reliable to occur. How to measure of MTR crowding, e.g. weighting the gap between the busy time, the standard (i.e. objective) and the perceived (i.e. subjective) metrics. We are not in a position to definitely map the two dimensions, which is a crucial requirement for translating objective improvements into equivalent subjective gains that then can be applied, willingness to pay estimates MTR ticket fares to obtain the additional MTR passenger benefits of MTR public transportation investment to any terminal stations. Because MTR crowding has a negative impact on passengers in terms of psychological on emotional distress. MTR passengers are willing to stand for up to 20 minutes of the service is fast and reliable. However crowding outweighed these benefits from a MTR passenger's perpective, experienced crowding leads a increased dissatisfaction. e.g. stress and less privacy during who needs to stand up in MTR. Due to there are no enough places to supply to them to stand up in MTR. If the MTR trip time was longer time between the passenger's terminals, who will feel more dissatisfaction and it will cause who feels whether who ought need to choose to catch other transportation tools to substitute MTR next time. e.g. bus, train, tram, ferry, taxi etc. So, from an operator's perspective, the MTR service frequency or MTR size is significantly influenced by the level of ridership, which sends a signal to respond if the monitored crowding level exceeds the benchmark standard in the busy time. e.g. in the morning time or at the night time, the students or employment people who need to go to schools or offices (working places). The locations of different places between MTR terminals and crowding are regarded as a key service attribute for MTR pubic transportation along with other factors, such as travelling time and reliability, e.g. service quality, none engineering machines are broken to cause MTR stops suddenly.

Given the increasing importance of crowding on both the disutility to existing MTR public transportation users and the influence to it. MTR passenger can choose to use either the MTR public public transportation or other public transportation. It is timely to review the MTR current measures of crowding defined by transportation authorities. MTR operators ought evaluate whether they apporpriately reflect MTR each traveler experiences and perceptions of crowding in busy (peak) time. I suggest that MTR needs to buy other underground trains to supply to the busy (peak) time passengers to let them have enough seats to sit down, so who do not need to stand up in any MTR underground trains when they catch MTR underground trains in busy time. It aims to let who are willingness to pay the estimation of reasonable ticket fares to compare the other kinds of transportation tools in the busy (peak) time.

● What is the crowding difference between train and MTR underground train.

In fact, crowding won't be happened to brother these transportation tools easily in the busy time and non busy time both. e.g. bus, taxi, train, tram, ferry. Because passengers can not choose to stand up in these transportation tools easily, due to these transportation tools have no enough areas (spaces) to let them to stand up easily . So, the crowding will be avoided to occur in these tranportation tools usually. Otherwise, MTR will have many passengers who can choose to stand up because MTR design of length is very long and it has enough areas (places) to let passengers to choose to stand up, even there have none any seats are provided to let them to sit down. So, MTR passengers will feel more dissatisfaction and crowding easily, especial in any peak (busy) time every day.

Comparing to bus, much more diverse crowding measures are defined in the passenger rail industry. For passenger, different specifications for measuring crowding are found across countries and even within a country. For example, rail crowding measures in the UK, the passengers in excess of capacity is crowding measure that applies to all London and South east operators weekday train services at a London terminus during the morning peak from 0700 to 09: 59 , and those departing during the afternoon peak from 16:00 to 18:59 (office of rail regulation 2011 year). The overall PIXC figure is considered the planned standard class capacity of each train service as well as the actual number of standard class passengers on the service at the critical point. i.e. the location on a trains of standard class passengers that surpass the planned capacity as the difference between the number of actual passengers and the capacity of the train divided by the number of passenger is within the capacity . So, it seems train and MTR underground public transportaton tools had been encountering the crowding problems in peak time, the difference in train passengers need to wait next train or more train arrival is who doesn't plan to enter the train, when who discovers the current train has no seats to provide to them to sit down in whose trip. Otherwise, MTR passengers can choose either to stand up within the large areas (places) if who discovered there are no any seats to provide to them to sit down or who can wait the next MTR arrival in order to who can sit down. It seems MTR transportation tool crowding environment includes in waiting platform and inside of the MTR underground train. Otherwise, train transportation tool crowding environment only includes the waiting platform and the passengers will not have crowding feeling inside of the train, due to none of passengers choose to stand up inside any trains because any train inside has no enough places to let them to stand up.

● How MTR can attract many passengers.

On the commuter departure time choice of any reference point researching hand, the departure time decisions of communters are of fundamental importance of peak period MTR traffic congestion. However, whether on the demand side, MTR underground train congestion relief measures, such as MTR ticket fare to every terminal station needs to be charged cheaper fare or discount fare in the peak (busy) time every day. To aim to attract many passengers to choose to catch MTR Underground train public transportation tools, substitute to choose other public transportation tools in the peak time.

Over the past decades, there have been very active research efforts in the departure time problem, both in econometric modeling and dynamic user equilibrium fields. Although, these works provide valuable insights into dynamic commuter decision making, they do not identify the commuters' response to gains and losses related to whole actual arrival time to reference points who may have relative. The appliability of the reference point hypothesis of prospect theory to the commuter's departure time decision making to obtain a better understanding of how departure time choice in MTR platform during their waiting underground train arrival time. However, every MTR underground train actual arrival time and deviation variables related to reference points (gains and losses) are the key factors in the departure time choice model. How the MTR underground train of every communter's daily departure time decision can be modelled when the reference point hypothesis of prospect theory. The MTR underground train's schedule delay is defined as the difference between the preferred arrival time (PAT) and the actual arrival time (AT) for a given MTR commuter. In a daily MTR commute, a commuter in the indifference band actual arrival time is an essential feature of MTR schedule study. Two reference points are the earliest acceptable arrival time and the work starting time for a given

MTR platform waiting passengers. In psychological view point, prospect theory proposes that the displeasure of a loss is perceived or greater than the pleasure of a gain of the same attitude and therefore, the value function is stronger for losses than gains.

To conclude, it seems that if MTR waiting passengers need not spend long time to wait underground train arrival in platform and it can provide seats to let them to sit down in the busy (peak) crowding time. It will make them to feel pleasure, even the MTR ticket fare is not fair and reasonable to charge higher fare to compare other kinds of public transportation tools fares. So the peak waiting time factor can influence the passengers to choose other kind of transportation tools to catch easily. Moreover, MTR's two reference points are the earliest role. Similarly a loss is observed when the MTR platform waiting commuter experiences or actual arrival time which is beyond that the MTR schedule time. Due to that a MTR waiting commuter is as an early side arrival of whose actual arrival time is earlier than whose preferred arrival time.

SEVEN

AIRLINE TRANSPORT SERVICE INDUSTRY

● How positive or negative social change can influence any airlines' air ticket prices to be risen or fallen.

We are entering globalization. In Special, airline transportation demands are also increasing, due to many travelers need to catch planes to travel as well as many cargoes need to be carried to planes to transport to different countries to sell. It seems aviation transportation industry is important to influence the health of the global economy growth nowadays. However, ignorance of internal or external market dynamics, catching travelers business can be detrimental to airline profitability more than carrying cargoes business. Because the demands of travelling different countries' travelers' consumption are still more than the demands of businessmen carrying cargoes in any countries every year. So, the global GDP of travelling income sector is still have the important position to any country nowadays. How can positive or negative social change influence any airlines' air ticket prices to be risen or fallen? In fact, the increase in petroleum price can have chance to affect airlines in a negative manner because increased oil prices have resulted in the reduction of services operations, the number of airline schedules flights, even airline bankruptcies. Whether inflation, terrorism, oil price, bank interest rate etc. external factors which factor has the most influential to cause the bad effects to cause airline industry share price reducing or reducing air ticket price or decreasing traveler numbers. To support this hypotheses, this are my research questions, such as : Does a combination of terrorism and price of petroleum significantly influence airline profit changing mostly? The alternative hypothesis was whether a significant relationship exists between terrorism, price of petroleum and airline profitability more than other factors, such as inflation, bank interest rate or air ticket price changing of these factors influence. I shall indicate that the first assumption was that terrorism has a negative effect on airline profitability and another assumption was that only external factors as oil prices or terrorism affect airline profitability.

● What is the relationship of oil price and terrorism to airline industry? However the effects of oil price and terrorism on airline profitability was limited to a regional perspective, e.g. the terrorism attack of plane crash event to USA on 11 Sept. After the terrorism attack happened on USA 11 Sept. incident of terrorism attack was restricted to events of skyjacking, attacks on oil production, refinery and distribution. Other types of terrorist activities, such as attacks on financial targets or senior government officials could have an adverse effect on the petroleum and airline industry. I think the disruption of the production or distribution of petroleum because of incidents of terrorism was costly in terms of loss of business and the inflationary effect on fuel dependent products or services. In fact, some airlines have adopted more fuel saving technology, so whose fuel consumption would not use more than other non fuel saving technology airlines. It seems fuel price increasing will not be the only factor to influence the airline industry's traveler numbers decreasing. However, due to some airlines which have fuel saving technology, so which can avoid to use more fuel to provide planes to use and which fuel costs will be reduced, then which can provide cheaper air ticket fare prices to compare the non fuel saving technology airlines. The result will cause some airlines will lose travelling customers in this global airline travelling market, also the non fuel saving technology airlines need to renew their fuel technology if which want to keep their competitive abilities to avoid to close down their businesses.

Also, I shall indicate the financial risk of airline industry evidence from Cathay Pacific airways and China airlines against key determinants of which include interest rate, exchange rate and fuel price risk for the period of January 1996 year to December 2011 year. During this period, these key external factors which were the most serious influence to cause these two airlines choose to change their strategic behaviors. Due to any these financial risks is difficult to predict and it was also changing often, these factors will also affect any airlines stock returns which arise from changing economic conditions, e.g. fuel price movements and fluctuations in exchange rates. These external unpredicted changing factors will attribute to the air tickets cyclical demand, capital investment, fixed costs of labor and landing rights to this global airline industry.

However, the relationship between fuel price and stock prices varies across economies. The effects of oil price changes in sub-sector indices, such as wood, paper and printing, insurance and electricity. In the past, on global stock exchange market was positively significant in 2011 year. Otherwise, with respect to the U.S.A. aviation industry, some economists suggested that global airlines stock returns were negatively to percentage change in fuel prices related to any airline firm value, e.g. Qantas and Air New Zealand were negatively share price growth to fuel price risk in the short term in the 2011 year.

● Why does airline self organization exist in airline industry?

However, there are some airlines which are the characteristic of self organization and they are present in that both of oil fuel production and providing flights service in airline industry. So, these self organization airlines can control the oil fuel price by themselves. However, self organization is also evident in efforts by businesses acts of terrorism against economic targets by adopting proactive steps, such as airline and airport security. So, it seems self organization airline can reduce the risk to avoid oil price raising and terrorism attacks in airline industry risk management sector. Beside, these self organization airlines which have high technology of fuel efficient aircrafts, the use of one aircraft model, the adoption of direct routes versus customer loyalty programs and other operational cost reductions are strategies for increased profitability. To solve oil price, terrorism etc. external risk to airline industry. Instead of high technology of fuel efficient aircrafts and self organization methods can solve terrorism attacks and oil price rising risks. However, I believe that there are other risks are caused to airline industry. The risks include such as user factor, such as culture, tradition, education ; economic factor, such as costs, human resources and macro economic factor, such as political stability, economic development, educational policy, health policy, environmental policy. However, these risks occurrences are resulting in the relationship of cause and effect events. These events are not directly observable. Such as, the complexity of relationship between terrorism and airline profitability. Hence, if global airline industry can predict when those risks occur to do protective strategic behavior. It is possible that which can understand why these risk events will occur and their protective strategic behaviors also influence their outcomes to be positive to avoid any external risk threats on the long term. However, I think hierarchy, airlines self organization efficiency methods which are as possible predictors of user preferences to avoid risk threat events to cause whose airline businesses failure occurrences in airline industry.

● Why tourism and airline industries have close relationship to influence their profitability between of them.

In my study, I suppose terrorism, profitability and the price of petroleum which had properties of distinct and interrelated close relationship. Moreover, these variables (terrorism, profitability and the price of petroleum) displayed differentiation, self replication, efficiency and hierarchy which can cause risk events to airline industry. However, I also think the other internal and external threat factors of airline industry, such as inflation, bank interest rate, business model, service quality, airline fuel or plane engine technology, air ticket pricing, brand loyalty, airline strategic management, government policy and fuel hedging of these factors which can also raise the risks to threaten any airlines existence in airline industry.

There are two basic business models in airline industry. They are network (full service) and low cost (discount) carriers. The network carrier model employs diversification strategy by increased domestic destinations, serving international routes, providing diverse seating arrangements (business, economy and first class), maintaining a complex system of offering high quality service. Otherwise, low cost (discount) airlines focus on lower air fares. To keep operating costs down, discount airlines offer shorter routes and provide point-to-point destinations rather than through sophisticated flights are primarily in domestic destinations. So, discount airlines operate a common model aircraft fleet, offer a single seating arrangement and cheaper flight services offered to compare network airlines. However, these two basic business models have their unique competitive abilities to provide any airlines existence in airline industry nowadays.

In fact, natural resource of oil is decreasing in our earth. But as the same time, human demand is increasing and oil supply is decreasing, so it also causes the oil fuel price is increasing to supply to airline industry. It influences not only to airline industry, it also impacts of higher oil fuel price to tourism, such as expansion of airports are made based on expected demand increase. Tourism has been proven to many adverse events, including terrorism, flight disruptions. Beside, the bad natural climate change influences, such as the volcanic ash cloud event occurred in April 2010 year. So, airline industry need to concern climate change because it will cause high fuel prices indirectly. For example, the event occurred the extreme increase in operating costs for airlines in 2008 year, due to unprecedented prices for aviation fuel also meant, that despite the introduction of fuel charges, so this event causes the global airline industry recorded losses seriously. Even if alternative fuels become commercially available for airlines which are still likely to be more expensive than present aviation fuel.

Higher airfares in the future are likely to lead to reduction in travel and cause tourists to shift from more distant to closer destination. When some of the economic responses to higher oil prices are obvious assessing the overall economic impacts on tourism is difficult. However, long term changes in global oil price rises will be similar to global changes in other commodity prices, exchange rates and income. It is therefore important to consider the impact of high oil prices on tourism from a general equilibrium perspective rather than relying only on bottom partial equilibrium approaches.

However, I believe tourism and airline industries have close relationship, such as tourism and airline industries are likely to suffer in an environment of high oil prices. Given that tourism destinations receive tourists from a range of origins, it would be useful to understand of some countries are increasing oil prices than others. Such as the net oil importing countries are selling higher oil prices than oil exporting countries generally. For example, New Zealand is an oil import country to provide planes for international visitor arrivals, so its oil fuel price is usually higher to charge to NZ airlines because any NZ airlines need to pay to foreign countries to buy any oil more expensive price. So, NZ airlines usually charge higher airfares to its visitors to compare the other exporting oil countries' airlines.

In economic theory, on income effects indicate negative impacts on tourism demand, the exact effects of higher oil fuel prices for specific destinations are far from clear. However, airline industry's different market segments show different sensitivities to air ticket fares changes. On the first hand, if the visitors are long destinations generally wealthier than average and therefore potentially less affected, as energy costs would be a smaller proportion of their income compared will be those from less wealthy groups. On the second hand, oil prices don't translate into higher transport costs especially not on air routes that are highly competitive and that are maintained for strategic reasons. On the third hand, many other factors shape tourists' decision making, including emotion drivers or those related to images, fashions and perceptions. Increasing environmental protection awareness of tourists could also be an important factor to influence tourism consumption, instead of oil fuel price raising causes air ticket fares raising factor to reduce traveler numbers. However, oil price raising reason causes also due to high use of cars, vans and domestic air transport in some countries, e.g. Hong Kong, China countries, there are many people like to buy cars to drive. So, the private driver numbers are increasing demand to cause these countries' oil fuel prices raise in the short time suddenly.

● Why oil fuel raising price factor can cause risk to airline.

In long run, implications of changes to supply and demand side conditions of oil fuel energy may differ qualitatively. For example, due to investment responses of producers, consumers and governments in alternative energy sources and more energy efficient plants, vehicles are supplied in order to achieve oil fuel price can't be risen seriously. However, I believe oil fuel rising charge will be an important factor to influence global airline ticket fares to be also increased. Firstly, on the bank interest changing factor, e.g. bank interest rate rising which only attract more bank saving. But it can not influence the bank savers who choose to reduce relax time to go to other countries travelling. Otherwise, when the bank savers can save more money to earn higher interest in banks, who will prefer to choose to use their saving to consume travelling. Due to who can earn higher interest rate after a period of saving time. So, I believe who behavioral travelling consumption will be raised when the banks will raise interest rate, then the bank savers won't choose to save more money in banks. So it is possible that who will withdraw more money to consume to go to travelling from banks. It seems bank interest rate changing won't influence bank savers' behavioral travelling consumption to be reduced. Secondly, on the exchange rate changing factor, although any country's exchange changing will cause other countries' money value to be fallen down or risen up. However, it won't influence any travelers' behavioral consumption to be reduced seriously. Although, it is possible that the traveler won't spend too much to go to shopping when who travel to the another country and arrive the country. But, it is not possible to influence the traveler decides to reduce consumption to buy any air ticket to go to travelling. Thirdly, any country inflation also can not reduce travelers' travelling consumption easily because inflation can influence consumers who choose to buy cheaper foods and clothing and reduce entertainments in their every day life. But, one country's inflation can not influence it's citizen do not spend much travelling expenditure because travelers only spend one time or two times of travelling every year usually. So, the travelling expenditure rate of any households is not too much to compare daily essential expenditure. So, it seems that bank interest rate and exchange rate changing and inflation won't influence any travelers' travelling consumption of decisions to be reduced easily. Otherwise, if the oil fuel price raises too much, then global airlines' cost will be raised. So, the airlines only choose to increase their air fare prices to aim to avoid loss possibly. It seems that oil fuel price has direct influence airline income.

● Methods to solve rising air fare prices demand.

I. Why will biofuels energy be demanded ?

I suggest these methods how to avoid the oil raising price factor to cause airline air fare prices to be risen to lead the risk of traveler numbers to be reduced. The first method: Whether aviation fuel markets will have what benefits from biofuels supply to planes. I shall refer the scope includes trends in jet fuel price, airline response to fuel price, increases and volatility and environmental goals for aviation. The aviation fuel supply industry includes production, distribution and consumption of aviation fuel and it outlines players in the aviation fuel supply chain. For example, at each airport, fuel supply chain organization and fuel sourcing could differ with regard to the role of oil companies, airlines, airport owners and operators and airport service companies. However, major jet fuel purchasers are airlines, general aviation operators, corporate aviation and the military, with most of the jet fuel in global different countries demanders being used for domestic commercial and civilian flights carrying passengers, cargos or both. Commercial aviation fuel efficiency has improved dramatically over time, largely due to aircraft and engine upgrades and operational and air traffic control improvements. So, it seems that fuel supply factor can influence airline fare prices majorly. However, jet fuel prices generally correlate with prices of crude oil and other refined petroleum products, such as diesel. So, increasing prices and the persistent price volatility of jet fuel markets import airline industry finances in any countries. However, airlines use various strategies to manage aviation fuel price certainty, including financial hedges, increased vertical integration and adjustments in aircraft utilization and size to avoid the jet fuel raising price risk. Investments in alternative aviation fuel could be a mechanism to diversity expose to the price of petroleum. It seems the use of alternative aviation fuel would serve to diversify the fuel mix to reduce the risk of jet fuel monopoly raising price threat. If a diversified fuel mix were to avoid either fuel raising price in short term or to avoid fuel raising price in long term. Potential benefits include reduced actual fuel costs from only choice of jet fuel supply increased price certainty and lessened fuel costs. This diversify could allow airlines to become more consistently profitable and to make other investments in their businesses.

So, biofuels have potential to meet aviation industry needs, possibly including managing risks of upward fuel price trends and fuel price volatility and avoid risks with greenhouse gas emissions. So, the aviation fuels market could use biofuels to reduce greenhouse gas emission and mitigate long-term upward price trends, fuel price volatility or both. What are the challenges of high priced oil for aviation? In fact, nowadays not the resources of oil as such, but much more the insecurity of supply, due to geopolitical instability in combination with a tight oil market makes a scenario with much higher oil prices than the world is currently experiencing not unlikely. Aviation is completely dependent upon oil as its fuel source. Since no practical energy substitute is readily available for commercial aviation, a scarcity of petroleum relative to demand will present a major aviation policy. In addition, efficiency gains, due to operational measures and new aircraft medium term. In particular, it has been demonstrated that the annual reduction rate in fuel consumption traffic unit is not a constant, but is itself also falling, in contrast to past estimates. So, a high-priced oil scenario will have severe consequences for demand, airline revenues, the competitive position of airports and eventually airline networks, strategies and fleet development. In particular, transfer demand, short-haul and leisure traffic can be expected to be heavily affected by high oil prices, due to their relative high price sensitivity. So, different countries' governments or/and airlines are valuable to research another new and potential biofuel energy to substitute oil energy to supply our planes to reduce the threat of oil monopoly supply to influence the cause of air fare raising prices. Because the elasticity is very high to travelers, when the travelers feel air fares are rising high or even low level to influence travelers who will choose not to buy the air tickets to go to travel easily.

Whether will the fuel (oil based inputs) risk be high to compare other costs, e.g. engineering maintenance, employees salaries, general cleaning, security office expenses etc. expenditures to airlines? If the probability-weighted upside effect on firm value when a risk is resolved favorably is greater the risk than the probability-weighted downside effect if the risk is resolved badly, then expected value work not be enhanced by hedging. So, the risk will be resolved badly to any commercial airlines. Airlines are an interesting case because the direct effect of source of risk resides squarely within the no offset in revenue functions (unlike for oil producers, for example), so value effects from costs feed directly into equity value. Most directly, the risk source is fuel costs to commercial airlines. Jet fuel is of course, a mix product of crude oil, so airlines indirectly face oil price risk. There are reasons to expect that airlines' fuel costs might to convex in oil price (i.e. absent any hedging). For example, oil prices, being generally pro-cyclical in recent times, tend to be highest when airline demand is strong. Airlines are therefore apt to use more high priced fuel than low-priced fuel over time. Airlines can raise air fare benefit is limited by the elasticity of demand. Also, cost functions could be influenced from fuel cost corresponds to upturns in economic activity overall (due to demand pressures on oil related prices), so it causes that airline's capacity delivers their services given their level of fixed capital. The essence of airlines basis risk in the case of jet fuel is essentially the time profile of the refining margin between crude and jet fuel, or the time profile of the price differential between other refined distillates and jet fuel. Thus, it is far from clear that risk management with oil is sure to add value to any airlines. It seems the impact of airline energy and any countries' domestic or foreign airline passenger travel numbers which have direct close relationship.

II. Whether the relationship between terrorism and oil prices has close relationship.

Whether the relationship between terrorism and oil prices has close relationship. It needs to judge to determine if a combination of terrorism and the price of petroleum significantly predicted airline profitability and which variable whether the further period was the most significant between the terrorism occurrence and the price of petroleum influence. So, different countries' governments or airlines need to collect samples of financial records from which country's any airline commercial passengers and cargo airlines on costs of fuel and any airline profitability. Also, gathering the terrorism data were comparison of terrorist attacks on petroleum in oil-producing nations, and incidents of high jacking aboard any country's aircraft. When any countries' airlines or governments can judge whether the impact of airline energy and terrorism risk level is high or middle or low level. Then, which can use this sample data to measure how to do positive social change to whether to increase or reduce employment in commercial aviation industry, or ought need to invest other higher commercial activity in tourist and other travel related service businesses and when is the most right time to adopt of green technologies by the civil aviation manufacturing industry after the terrorism attacks occurrence to any country. It seems that any countries' governments or airlines which ought concern that the event of when the terrorism attacks will occur and gather past sample data to predict when the next time terrorism attacks event will be occurred and the risk will be high or middle or low level to influence global airline industry development.

III. What factors will influence airline industry's price elasticity of supply and demand?

In fact, the airline industry is largely dependent on the supply of the oil industry. Otherwise, the oil industry is inelastic. However, the increase or decrease of the price of airfare is directly related to the increase or decrease of the oil's price to fuel the aircrafts because there has no any new energy which can be substituted to oil fuel to airline industry. So, it seems oil fuel producers are monopolies to control its sale price to be raised easily. Another factor that can affect airline industry to be directly targeted by a tragedy brought about by terrorism. The past four years, from 2001 year to 2005 year, there had been at least $40 billion worth of losses in the airline industry because of the September 11 date terrorism attacks in 2000 year. There had been an expected and significant decrease in the demand for the airline industry services because of the attacks that involved planes hijacking and crashing into key locations like the World Trade Center and the Pentagon in USA. Although, terrorism attacks can bring risk to influence fuel price rising in airline industry. However, this risk occurrence to airline industry is only that after the terrorism attacks occurred. It is possible that terrorism attacks won't occur again in the future. Otherwise, our concerning ought be the greenhouse emissions and how it affects global warming. The air quality would be better once this new regulations are adopted. However, it would affect large airlines. So, it would increase the price of airfares because of economic fees that airline companies have to cover. Air pollution can give a negative impact on the domestic or oversea owned airline companies for long term. If airlines' planes can use clean fuel to fly, e.g. biofuel, then it will bring benefits to global airlines for long term. On the positive side, the environment would be healthier as the earth's temperature would rise, and greenhouse effect would be dramatically reduced. This positive effect can come at a cost that is greater than most people perceive. On the psychology view point on travelers, who will be more preferable to catch planes to go to different countries to travel, due to the chance of air pollution and global environmental warm issues will be reduced to low risk to influence our health if planes can use biofuel to be energy to fly in the future one day. It seems that spending expenditure to research other non polluted biofuel new energy is one solvable method to global airline industry in the future. To solve, any airlines or countries' governments or oil producers ought choose to spend more time to research new biofuel. Otherwise, the predicting when terrorism attacks event will be occurred, it is more difficult to predict the time more than researching to produce new biofuel energy method in the future. So, I recommend that researching the new biofuel energy or other kinds of energy to substitute the oil energy is the urgent behavioral economy which the airlines or oil producers or different countries' governments which need to concern nowadays.

EIGHT

SPACE TECHNOLOGICAL INDUSTRY

● Introduction

When discussing the advancement of space science and space technology, most people think about deep space flights, lunar stations, and thrilling outer space adventures. The fact is that the majority of the human technology in space, which consists of interconnected satellites, points towards Earth, and is used to provide services for and fulfil the goals of people on planet Earth. Over the next decade, there will be an increased need for innovative Earth information systems to support the international space community's efforts to provide a robust infrastructure. Space exploration requires vast sums of money. Is the amount of money spent on space research justifiable? Could the money be better spent? There has always been considerable discussion about whether governments should spend tax payers' money on space research. In my view it is impossible to justify the amount of money spent on such projects. Generally speaking, the main reason for this position is that there are several areas in which the money could be invested better. The first point to make is that politicians have a responsibility to spend public money on projects that bring a benefit to the general public. This has not been the case with space research as most developments have been limited to helping astronauts in space or have been very specialised. For example, it is not of great value to the general public that we now have pens and biros that can write upside down. This does not merit the huge amount of money spent. Thus, I feel it is very difficult to justify whether space exploration is value to invest or not at present. We need to wait time to observe whether what the main rewards or benefits to human in the future. However, I shall indicate what benefits human can get from any products or services of space exploration in this book.

A conceptualization of space exploration

Since the early 1970 year, the social sciences concern the process of globalization. Brennan (2011) explained " that globalization means the new international division of labor, changing forms of industrial organization and processes of urban-regional restructuring to transformations in the nature of state power, civil society, citizenship, democracy, nationalism, localities and architectural forms among many others. However, globalization research includes geographical concepts, such as space-time compression, space of flows, space of places, globalization , localization and scape, among many other terms ." Hence, the conceptualization of space exploration can relate to globalization by the channel e.g. the internet, a symbol that we are all connected and nobody is quite in charge as well as everyone in the world is affected, directly or indirectly. Also by this new Global investment in satellite navigation systems was extensive in the 2000 year. The USA with the GPS system. In particular, the space exploration means the space market has expand into new niche sector: Space tourism and travel, mining of resources, manufacturing opportunities , satellite technology all represent a shift toward privatization of the sphere. The new century is an important time in the history of space, not just for science, but in the opportunities it offers for business enterprise and commercialization. Human being are no longer in pursuit of progress and dreams of a high technological, science fiction life, they will use space technology to solve problems on Earth and to improve their quality of life despite limited financial resources.

Again, Brenna (2011) showed "Today, USA, Russia etc. countries are the world's super-powers at the time were engaged in the space race. They believe exploration and application of Earth orbital space become serious resources of national development and real advancement of people's living standards." The present day space industry has evolved from the romanticism of the 1960s and 1970s, when putting a human being on the moon captured the imagination of the world. Now, a multi-pronged approach to space exploration is attempting to address environment issues, advance technology and industry, and cater for the next generation of holiday makers the space tourists. A number of factors have contributed to the globalization of the space industry. Political changes in the 1990s and the end of the space race meant that almost all trading nations, function with market based economies and their trade polices have tended to encourage free market between nations. The globalization of the space industry has been further encouraged by technical standardization between countries. Most governments actively seek to encourage global operators to base themselves in their countries (namely, the USA space infrastructure, Russian know how, Brazilian lower launch costs). Yip (2003) cities "decreasing costs, globalization, scale economies, sourcing efficiencies as offering the potential for competitive advantage to some countries." A recent report from the Futron Corporation (2009) addresses strategic private questions about space power and competitiveness:

● What are the core measure of space competition?

● Is space nationalism on the rise, and if so, what are the implications?

● What are the implications of multi-polar space community?

● What are the economic consequences of a commercial space environment based on multiple international providers of key technologies, systems and services?

Hertzfeld (2007) has described how space power can be viewed from a commercial perspective in two ways. "The first is economic: Encouragement of USA space ventures to be dominant in the world marketplace, either through the creation of a monopoly by market dominance. The second is aggressively denying others access or interfering with the operations of foreign space assets. " Thus, it is possible that space exploration can stimulate the economy via job creation and the possibility of products entering future potential economic aspect of two civilian application of space technologies: communications and meteorology. Another author's opinion, Taraseko (1996) has classified "Russian space systems according to the missions performed. These systems can be sub-divided into space weapons, space surveillance and intelligence systems, support systems and scientific systems ." He implied Russian will concentrate on manufacturing space weapons , then it will also sell space weapons to global finally. I think space exploration will have military and civil two aspects, instead of space tourism. Thus, on space system military aspect, it includes space weapons, space to Earth anti- satellite, early warning. Beside, on space system civil aspect, it includes support and applied communications, navigation, mapping, meteorological remote sensing and scientific research. It implies 'Globalization' will be cooperated by different main space leaders who will be carrying on space exploration activities in the future.

The benefits and Values are managed to international
cooperation in space exploration

The 1960's brought new advancements for all of Earth. Machines and men were sent into space, and this sparked a new government agency, called NASA. Space was a new frontier, and virtually everyone was interested in exploring it. Over the years, the interest in space exploration has weakened, and NASA was almost terminated from existence, although there have been many advancements in it over that time. Space exploration should continue because it could help solve many problems on Earth, such as overpopulation and lack of resources. Exploration of the final frontier must continue in order for human life to continue to international cooperation in space exploration. International cooperation in space exploration has the potential to provide significant benefits to all participants, particularly if managed well. Benefits in the form of monetary efficiency, raising economy development and workforce stability will accrue to those partners who choose to approach space exploration as a mutually beneficial to raise employment.

The first utility benefit, it is common knowledge that international cooperation in space exploration has the potential to reduce a partner's costs by spreading the burden to other nations. Although, additional overhead costs increase the overall cost to among partners. As per-partner cost decreases, pre-partner utility increases. Space exploration has proven to be an expensive activity.

The second goodwill benefit, the more countries participate, the higher will be the utility. As such, Indian, Russia and China countries participation in joint space exploration would send a strong signal to the world of good USA-Indian and Russian and Chinese friendly relations and increases political sustainability. So, these countries space exploration of cooperation which will help them to build friendship of intangible benefits.

The final raising employment benefit, international cooperation can enable workforce stability, one way politicians measure the benefits of a large space exploration program is in terms of the number of jobs and amount of revenue. For example, both the space shuttle and space exploration programs employ workers across the country and serve as a source of revenue to the district of many numbers of congress. The space exploration program also employs enough people to attract the attention of the president. The loss of these jobs and revenue streams would constitute a large loss in utility for both administration and congress. Nevertheless, the aerospace industry must continually engage in advocacy activities to ensure that politicians are made aware of this fact. As such, if either the space shuttle or space exploration programs were to grow to employ more people, an increase in the perceived utility lost in the event of a cancellation of the space exploration program would only result of the growth were significant enough to attract political attention. Thus, positive utility for space exploration programmatic expansion only exists when a supporting coalition may be identified. As such, additional employment doesn't strictly deliver positive utility loss in the event of any space jobs are lost and utility is decreased, there is no additional positive utility to reinstating those jobs. Rather, the threat of the loss of utility inherent in the loss of employment can only serve as a deterrent. Such, employment space exploration programs therefore act in a manner similar to an addiction. Thus on the final employment benefit analysis, international cooperation might seem to decrease employment in the United States, because foreign nations are building components that might otherwise be constructed in the United States. In practice, those who are employed may see more stability in their jobs due to the twin utility losses associated with employment termination. In effect, employment has no impact on utility unless it changes. The stability provided by international cooperation will ensure that the associated utility is at least likely to decrease.

●

The impact of space exploration activities upon society.

As the 21st. century gets further underway, the impact of space activities upon the welfare of humanity will only increase. The period between 1957 yr. and 1991 yr. saw the space age with flights to the planets, footprints on the moon and global communications; even military space exploration. In the not clean solar energy from space powering our industries as well as heating and lighting our homes. Our nuclear waste may be safely and inexpensively disposed of by being carried up a space Elevator and released towards Earth Orbit or on the Moon. We may carry out the development of a multi-planet economy. In addition to the knowledge that space exploration has already delivered , space technologies have become integrated into everyday life so deeply that modern society could not function without them.

Weather, telecommunications, environmental analysis and national security are only the most obvious space technologies that humanity relies on, and transfers from space to non space sectors provide many additional indirect benefits. The basic activities required to develop and maintain the fundamental elements on which a space policy depends for its implementation (access to space, the technology base, industrial capabilities, ground facilities); the activities of sciences and human and robotic exploration ; and utilitarian activities are developing space systems to support public services , such as meteorology, environment, natural disaster prediction management, online education studying, wind, nuclear and water energy and agriculture growing and plant breeding research and commercial offering , such as distance long phone , internet , mobile telecommunications, GPS navigation and imagery for the benefit of the citizen. Thus the impact of space activities upon society has largely been measured I numerical terms. How many spacecraft have been launched by a given country? How many phone calls are made over a satellite? How many lives could be saved by hurricane watching satellites? How much money was spent on space within a given country or by a corporation? The problem with this approach is that generally, the value to humanity is not measured and the value and benefits of such space activities must be justified. For the purposes of such space exploration technologies and researching new materials become cheap enough or feasible enough to do so.

The aims of space exploration include one world perspective, challenges for life , knowledge development, educational stimulation, communications for all revitalization of the human spirit after and contributing ,such as distance learning. On the education hand, the stimulation of education and proactive outreach has been a historic strengths of the space exploration. On the communication hand, communications for all revitalization, such as the space field has matured, the innate human desire to communicate has grown ever more significant. The need to transmit data, information and knowledge. For example, the communication with a spacecraft beyond the solar system or with a friend by mobile phone. Though television, we can watch wars in real time as soldiers and hurt people who are being conducted on the ground, we can witness the sport players at the Olympic Games, we listen to latest news on the radio when driving in our cars. The ability to communicate easily and quickly with ships at seas ,aircrafts in mid-flight or a relative on the other side communications technologies developed for space. On the one world perspective hand, the people of the world saw the blue marble of the Earth as on Earth rise from the window of Apollo 8. The realization is that humanity can view itself in a new light. Humankind has made important in the peaceful exploration if outer space, and this has changed our lives here on Earth for the better new perspective and gain scientific knowledge. Hence, space technology gives benefits that have as to solve social and economic challenges, including poverty, environmental protection and bad weather disaster prediction.

Charles B. (2012) wrote here's an example: in 2012, NASA administrator Charles Bolden published a blog post about the Curiosity Mars rover landing, which was picked up by the White House website. "It's also important to remember that the $2.5 billion investment made in this project was not spent on Mars, but right here on Earth, supporting more than 7,000 jobs in at least 31 states." Another benefit is education, such as NASA's education office has three goals: making the workforce stronger, encouraging students to pursue STEM careers (science, technology, engineering and mathematics), and "engaging Americans in NASA's mission." Other space agencies also have education components to assist with requirements in their own countries. It's also fair to say the public affairs office for NASA and other agencies play roles in education, although they also talk about topics such as missions in progress. But it's hard to figure out how well the education efforts translate into inspiring students, according to a National Research Council report on NASA's primary and secondary education program in 2008. Among other criticisms, the program was cited as unstable (as it needs to change with political priorities) and there was little "rigorous evaluation" of its effectiveness. But NASA's emphasis on science and discovery was also praised. Finally, space industry can bring intangible benefits, such as added to this host of business-like benefits, of course, are the intangibles. What sort of value can you place on better understanding the universe? Think of finding methane on Mars, or discovering a planet, or constructing the International Space Station to do long-term exploration studies. Each has a cost associated with it, but with each also comes a smidgeon of knowledge we can add to the encyclopedia of the human race. Thus, there also are benefits that may be we cannot anticipate ahead of time. The Search for Extraterrestrial Intelligence (SETI) is a network that advocates looking for life around the universe, likely because communicating with beings outside of Earth could bring us some benefit. And perhaps there is another space-related discovery just around the corner that will change our lives drastically. Earth-observation satellites, for example, have been used successfully in Africa, Asia and Latin America to detect the risk of outbreaks of malaria and other infectious diseases. Satellite communications are being used in several developing nations to provide health services and distance learning to rural communities and to relay information for the management of land, ocean and fresh water resources. Space exploration creates space travelling dreams and imagination (particularly in science fiction and the arts) and stimulated research in space , on space and from space. These activities impacted strongly society by providing a key clarification between science, theology and imagination that lead to a better knowledge of the Universe and its evolution and thus of the actual place of humans within it. They discovered that they are all passengers on one complex spaceship that has to be taken care of more seriously, impacting dramatically on their behavior. Space exploration has forces us to recognize how to solve the challenge of how we shall balance population, fossil resources,resources, sustainable resources, even enouraging discover of DNA science research from space alive. Therefore, space activity by itself is impacting society by giving human a different perspective, on giving another 'eye' to look at this world, our culture and everyday life.

●

The benefits are stemming from space exploration
There are many reasons that space exploration should continue. If Earth ever becomes too overpopulated or over polluted, then perhaps people can move to Mars. The world population in 1970yr. was approximately 4 billion people, and is currently nearly 6 billion people. The world population in 2015yr. is estimated to be 7 billion people. There is a possibility that there are useful resources on Mars. Scientists have found ice and some other clues, such as craters, volcanoes, and valleys, that have led them to believe that there was once life on Mars. However, I shall indicate the technological innovation and cultural and inspiration and new opportunities for job creation and weather prediction and global space economy and global space economy benefits are stemming from space exploration as below:
On technological innovation aspect, there are numerous cases of societal befits linked to new knowledge and technology from space explanation. Space exploration aims to research new outside Earth's useful natural resources to substitute our limited natural resources because our prediction

indicates that our limited natural resources, e.g. oil, gas etc. which will be spent to use all none of natural resources remain in our Earth one day in the future. Space exploration has contributed to many diverse aspects of every day life from solar panels to implantable heart monitors, from caner therapy to light-weight materials, and from water purification systems to improved computing systems and to a global search and rescue system, storage and recycling and waste management, advances robotics, health and medicine, transportation, engineering, computing and software, space systems innovaion and service resulting in higher performance and lower costs.

On cultural and inspiration aspect, space exploration it fulfill people;s producing fresh data about the solar system , thus brings us closer to answering profound questions that have asked for: What is the nature of the Universe ? Is there life elsewhere in the Universe? Knowledge derived from space exploration may also contribute to implementing policies for environmentally sustainable development.

On new opportunities for job creation aspect, new opportunities for job creation and economic growth are being created by private enterprises that are increasingly investing in make space exploration and seeking ways to make space exploration more affordable and reliable, profitable , such as medicine, computer science, weather prediction, communication etc. industries. Such as space science discoveries and technology encourages European company to launch a satellite based super fast broadband service serving clients in rural .Telecommunications systems which enables European industry to explore new ideas for satellite communications products and services, such as mobile phones and internet and GPS location search. Thus, telecommunication encourages UK Government to implement digital Britian policy to secure the UK's position as one of the world's leading digital knowledge economies. The most influence indicates space exploration can create many new jobs demand to provide to UK telecommunication industry indiectly and it can assist UK economic growth.

On weather prediction aspect, space based systems have made an impact on how human deal with the environment. Earth observations from space can follow weather pattence. They can provide an understanding of hurricane formation, so that early warning early images from space can show the basing routes for access into areas cut off by flooding and other environmental disaster. Such as weather forecast, advance our understanding of atmospheric dynamic and climate processes, wind speed is one of the biggest unknowns in understanding what influences climate. So studying the climates of our planetary weighbours also help us to better understand the Earth's climate. Such as launched in 2000 numbers uncovered our sister planets, extrordinary atmospheric system, revealing for example, a bizarre giant double hurricane system at the south pole. Venus is extremely hot and suffers from a runway greenhouse effects, so provides an extreme model for studies of global warning. Mars, which is much colder than the Earth is an example of what happens when a planet loses its atmosphere. Mars spacecraft is mapping, the planet and observations indicate that water has once abundant on the Mar surface. Mar could once have harboured life and may do so again if humans decide to colonise it.

On the global space economy aspect, space exploration requires in many different areas to work together to develop new capabilities, that operate reliably in a remote environment. It has advanced telecommunications, medical technology, weather forecasting, navigation, television, radio, computing etc. industries. As a direct result of the innovations, inventions and discoveries that have enabled us to explore space, our daily lives on Earth have changed profoundly. For example, space related products and services is that cost less compared to the convenience, efficiency, information, such as direct to home television and satellite radio m the use of space by broadcast and cable television, satellites also enable truly global internet communication service, long distance telephone service. GPS satellite signals allow users on lands on the see and in the air will inexperience GPS devices to determine their position and aided by computer maps, other satellite capabilities , such as remote sensing, plot a course to their destination. GPS navigation has been so successful and valuable that the europeann space is investing to develop its own GPS satellite, GPS signals also provide precision timing for financial and cell phone networks.

● Summary

The feasibility of promising space product applications include earth insiders and space outsiders both. The earth insiders include distance leaving and telemedicine, electronic commerce entertainment, location-based consumer services, location-based services of traffic management, land cover of precision farming, urban planning, exploration (oil, gas), disaster prevention, meteorology and climate change and monitoring polices etc. aspects. The space outsiders include adventure space tourism, in orbital services, solar or wind energy power satellites technology. It seems space technology invention can solve energy shortage, it can predict weather change to reduce wind or water natural disaster chance occurrence , it can let human to give cheap fares to catch space ships to go to space to travel, it can use satellites to use GPS to assist drivers to find locations to drive different places in the short time or to assist pilots to find locations in sky or to assist ship captains to find location in sea easily, it can use satellites to solve traffic jam to shorten distance leaving on the road, it can encourage to sell medicines or products from internet conveniently. I think space technology can assist other new technology businesses to contribute human need in the future, so I feel that the main country space technology players who are worth to spend time to invest to invent this space technology different businesses in the future.

● Bibliography

Brennan, L. & Vecchi, A., (2011). The Business Of Space, The Next Frontier Of International Competition. Palgrave Macmillan Press: USA, New York.

Charles B. (2012) Curiosity Takes Us Back to Mars the

WHITE HOUSE Available at: Date Of Publication: 6 Aug.

https://www.whitehouse.gov/blog/2012/08/06/curiosity-takes-us-back-mars

Futron Corporation (2009) Resource Centre. Available at:

http://www.futron.com/resource_centre/resource_cemtre.htm.

Hertzfeld, H.R. (2007) Globalization, Commercial Space And Space Power In the USA, Space Policy, Vol.32, no 4. November.

Tarasenko, M.V. (1996) Evolution Of The Soviet Space Industry, Acta Astronautica, Vol. 38, no. 4-8, pp. 667-73.

Yip, GS. (2003) Total Global Strategy II: Updated For The Internet And Service Era (Upper Saddle River, NT: Presentice-Hall).

www.ingramcontent.com/pod-product-compliance
Lightning Source LLC
Chambersburg PA
CBHW031144130726
47988CB00006B/2517